TAO TE CHING

Lao-tzu

tao te ching

LIBER CLVII

TRANSLATED,
WITH AN INTRODUCTION
AND COMMENTARY,
BY

KO HSÜAN

(ALEISTER CROWLEY)

THE EQUINOX
Volume Three Number Eight

Edited by Hymenaeus Beta

SAMUEL WEISER, INC.

York Beach, Maine

This edition first published in 1995 by
Samuel Weiser, Inc.
P.O. Box 612
York Beach ME 03910-0612

Library of Congress Cataloging-in-Publication Data
Lao-tzu.
    [Tao te ching. English]
    Tao te ching : Liber CLVII / translated, and introduced with a com-
mentary by Aleister Crowley.
        p.   cm.
    The Equinox ; v. 3, no. 8.
    Includes bibliographical references and index.
    ISBN 0-87728-846-1
    I. Crowley, Aleister, 1875–1947.   II. Title.
BL1900.L26E5   1995
299'.5142--dc20   95-22270
TS   CIP
ISSN 1050-2904

Cover illustration: Untitled watercolor by Austin Osman Spare. Courtesy Pennsylvania State University Library Special Collections. ©1995 Estate of Austin
Osman Spare.

Typeset in 11 point Monotype Plantin Light.
Printed in the United States of America.

00 99
10 9 8 9 7 6 5 4 3 2

Contents

Editor's Foreword

Do what thou wilt shall be the whole of the Law.

THIS BOOK needs no introduction, as Crowley has provided his own, a rare instance of this author introducing his own work in any detail.[1] Nor should the *Tao Te Ching* (*Daode jing*),[2] attributed to Lao-tzu (Laozi), need any introduction. It has long been the most frequently translated of Chinese classics, and the discovery of the early Ma-wang-tui texts in 1973 E.V. has inspired yet more. Still, a discussion of the spiritual background for Crowley's edition of this work and its appendix—the *Ch'ing-ching Ching* (*Qingjing jing*)—is relevant, as is an examination of his use of the names Ko Yüen (Ge Yuan) and Ko Hsüan (Ge Xuan).

Crowley was the first Western poet and non-Sinologist to "translate" from the Chinese classics, although Ezra Pound's *Confucian Analects* (1950) saw print first. He had a great affinity for Taoism, regarding China's civilization as the most developed in the world. He regretted that he never found a living teacher for Taoism as he had for other spiritual traditions. He relied instead on James Legge's translations, the standard references for generations but today largely superceded by new scholarship.[3] Wing-tsit Chan wrote of Legge's translation of the *Tao Te Ching* that "while generally correct, modern scholarship requires a new approach at many points."[4]

---

[1] Crowley also discusses his work on the *Tao Te Ching* in *The Confessions of Aleister Crowley*, abridged edition, pp. 836–837. See Selected References.

[2] The Wade-Giles method of Chinese transliteration is generally used in this edition. Except for common words (like Tao and Te), the Pinyin method, which serves as a guide to pronunciation, is given in parentheses on its first occurrence in the editorial matter. Scholars currently employ one or the other, but no single standard exists as yet.

[3] Legge's translation appeared in *The Texts of Taoism* in 1881; for this and other translations see Selected References under Lao-tzu.

[4] Wing-tsit Chan, *An Outline and an Annotated Bibliography of Chinese Philosophy* (New Haven: Far Eastern Publications, 1969), p. 162.

In his Introduction Crowley mentions his Great Magical Retirement on Esopus Island during the late summer of 1918.[5] Few details are known of this retirement (or spiritual retreat) as Charles Stansfeld Jones (Frater Achad), who joined Crowley for part of it, destroyed most of the records.[6] This is a great loss, as it was probably the spiritual high point of Crowley's time in the United States (1914–1919).

Crowley wrote his translations of both the *Tao Te Ching* and *Ch'ing-ching Ching* on Esopus Island. As he explains in his Introduction, the *Tao Te Ching* was translated with the assistance of a discarnate adept (what a Taoist would likely term an "immortal") named Amalantrah. Crowley had been in frequent astral communication with Amalantrah for almost nine months.[7]

Crowley recovered memories of many of his previous incarnations during this retreat, an experience that provided the basis for his later writings on the magical memory.[8] In several of these remembered incarnations Crowley had been a Master of the A∴A∴ (or Great White Brotherhood) who had voluntarily incarnated to advance human evolution.[9] In reviewing some of these memories in his *Confessions*, he wrote that he suffered spiritual amnesia for incarnations before the time of Mohammed, with one notable exception:

> I merely remember that I was Ko Hsüan, a disciple of Lao-tzu, the author of the *Ch'ing-ching Ching*, the Classic of Purity; which, by the way, I translated into English verse during this retirement. All I know is that somehow or other I made a "great miss," forfeited my Mastership, and had to climb the ladder again from the bottom.[10]

---

[5] This tiny island, usually styled "Æsopus Island" by Crowley, lies just off the eastern bank of the Hudson River near Staatsburg, New York.

[6] For Crowley's and Jones' relationship see the Prolegomenon to Crowley, *Liber CXI vel Aleph*, 2nd ed. See Selected References.

[7] Crowley's Esopus Island retirement was in part a continuation of "The Amalantrah Working," which began in January. The diary records ("Liber 729") only survive through April, and do not include the summer of 1918.

[8] Chapter 7 of Crowley's *Magick in Theory and Practice* (*Book 4, Part III*) includes a lengthy discussion of magical memory; see Selected References under *Book 4*. A fragment of the Esopus Island record survives as "A Record of Some of the 'Past Lives' of Aleister Crowley," *The Magical Link* VI(4) (new series), New York: O.T.O., winter 1992–3. See also Chap. 37 of Crowley's *Magick without Tears*, which discusses the magical memory and his writing of the *Tao Te Ching*.

[9] For details of the A∴A∴ see "One Star in Sight" in Crowley, *Magick (Book 4, Parts I–IV)*, Appendix II. See Selected References.

[10] Crowley, *The Confessions of Aleister Crowley*, abridged ed., p. 839.

It is unclear whether Crowley meant that he committed this "great miss" as Ko Hsüan or a later incarnation, but his choice of phrase is no accident—it is from *The Book of the Law* II:27:

> There is great danger in me; for who doth not understand these runes shall make a great miss. He shall fall down into the pit called Because, and there he shall perish with the dogs of Reason.

Crowley's account of his "Vision of Jupiter" of September 5 refers to just such a "great miss"—one with the potential to "hurl every Master of the Temple into the Abyss." The Vision of Jupiter was the climax of his Esopus Island retirement, and one of his most exalted visions, but usually overlooked as the diary excerpt in his *Confessions* is the only surviving record. Crowley, for whom spiritual candor was a watchword, notes that he "did not dare to write what it actually was," and it is not described in detail:

> 5.00 p.m. The meditation of this afternoon resulted in an initiation so stupendous that I dare not hint at its Word. It is the supreme secret of a Magus, and it is so awful that I tremble even now—two hours later and more—2.20 p.m. was the time—as I write concerning it. In a single instant I had the Key to the whole of the Chinese wisdom. In the light—momentary glimpse as it was—of this truth, all systems of religion and philosophy became absolutely puerile. Even the Law appears no more than a curious incident. I remain absolutely bewildered, blinded, knowing what blasting image lies in this shrine. It baffles me to understand how my brother Magi, knowing this, ever went on.
>
> I had only one foreshadowing of this Vision of Jupiter—for so I may call it!—and that was a *samādhi* which momentarily interrupted my concentration of *sammāsati*. This can only be described vaguely by saying that I obtained a reconciliation of two contraries of which "There is a discrimination between good and evil" is one.
>
> This experience has shaken me utterly; it has been a terrible struggle to force myself to this record. The secret comes along the Path of *aleph* to Chokmah. I could write it plainly in a few words of one syllable, and most people would not even notice it. But it has might to hurl every Master of the Temple into the Abyss, and to fling every adept of the Rose Cross down to the Qliphoth. No wonder One said that the *Book T* was in ashes in the Urn of a Magus! I can't see at all how it will affect me at present. Even the Way of the Tao looks idiotic—but then of course that's what it is! So I suppose that's it, all right. And its freedom, in an utterly fascinating and appalling sense, is beyond my fiercest conception.[11]

---

[11] *Ibid.*, p. 840.

Crowley nowhere explains how this Vision of Jupiter pertains to that sphere, but it is clearly a more deeply initiated exploration of spiritual realms only touched upon in the 5th Æthyr of *Liber 418, The Vision and the Voice*. This record confirms that Crowley's work with the Taoist classics had a profound experiential basis.

The *Ch'ing-ching Ching* is *The Classic of Purity and Stillness* — its full title *T'ai Shang Ch'ing-ching ching* reflects its traditional attribution to Lao-tzu (T'ai Shang Lao-chün), mentioned in the text as Lao-chün (Lao Gun). The attribution to Lao-tzu of Taoist texts of impossibly late periods was common practice.

James Legge ascribed its authorship to Ko Hsüan (Crowley's remembered Chinese incarnation), giving him the alternate name Ko Yüen, and attributing the period of composition to the Wu Dynasty (222–280 E.V.). Neither attribution reflects current scholarship, though modern experts differ on its period of composition; Eva Wong dates the *Ch'ing-ching Ching* to the end of the Six Dynasties Era (220–589 C.E.),[12] and Livia Kohn dates it more conservatively to the Sung (Song) dynasty (960–1260 E.V.), when it became prominent as a central liturgical text of Chüan-chen (Quanzhen, Complete Perfection) monastic Taoism.[13] Relying on Legge, Crowley cited Ko Yüen of the Wu dynasty as the author in the title page for his versification in its first edition.[14]

Ko Hsüan (164–244 E.V.) was a Taoist philosopher and alchemist of the late Han to early Three Kingdoms periods. Like many other early Taoist sages (not to mention Aleister Crowley!), Ko showed complete indifference to social norms. Legge noted that he was "represented as a worker of miracles; as addicted to intemperance, and very eccentric in his ways."[15] He would spend hot summer days at the bottom of a pond, drunk,[16] and Legge even repeats an account of him walking on water.

Legge was probably the only source of information concerning Ko Hsüan and his philosophy available to Crowley. Given his

---

[12] Eva Wong, trans., *Cultivating Stillness, A Taoist Manual for Transforming Body and Mind*, p. x. This is a translation of the *Ch'ing-ching Ching* with a commentary and introduction.

[13] Livia Kohn, *The Taoist Experience*, pp. 12, 24. Pages 25–29 include a translation of the *Ch'ing-ching Ching*.

[14] Ko Hsüan is cited as the author in the "Praemonstrance of A∴A∴," *The Equinox* III(1) (1919), p. 14. The erroneous reference in the title page is omitted in this edition.

[15] James Legge, *The Texts of Taoism*, Vol. II, p. 248.

[16] Holmes Welch, *Taoism, The Parting of the Way* (Boston: Beacon Press, 1966), p. 128.

identification with Ko Hsüan as an earlier incarnation, what is intriguing is not the handful of facts that Legge recorded, summarized above, but what Legge did *not* say. Crowley would almost certainly have considered the historical data given below a striking corroboration of his magical memory, confirming that his memory of Ko Hsüan was indeed that of a Master of A∴A∴ recalling an earlier incarnation as another.

Ko Hsüan was an early member of the Ko (or Ge) family, a South Chinese clan of "magico-technicians." Their techniques included astrological spiritism, the control of demons, ecstatic trance induction, visualization of deities, longevity practices, alchemy, clairvoyance (with and without magical mirrors), sacramental drugs, meditation and ritual. Many of these techniques were adopted by the school of Shang-ch'ing (Shangqing, Highest Clarity) founded by Yang Hsi (Yang Xi) in the fourth century E.V. Ko Hsüan's grandson was Ko Hung (Ge Hong, 261–341 E.V.), author of the *Pao P'u tzu* (*Baopuzi*), a principal text of early Taoist philosophy and alchemy. A later descendant, Ko Ch'ao-fu (Ge Chaofu) drew on Ko family tradition, Mahāyāna Buddhist doctrine and Highest Clarity teachings to formulate the Ling-pao (Lingbao, Numinous Treasure) school of Taoism in the late fourth to early fifth centuries E.V.

Ling-pao Taoism teaches that the immortals in the celestial hierarchy assist human adepts along the path of attainment. Some immortals pre-existed the creation of Heaven and Earth, and are purely spiritual beings that do not incarnate as human avatars but instead help humanity through intermediaries who, although originally created human, have achieved immortality and repeatedly incarnate to help others to attain.[17] The greatest of the pre-existent immortals is creator and ruler of Heaven and Earth, and dictates scriptures to these intermediaries at the beginning of each new world age, detailing the celestial hierarchy, rites of invocation, and means of individual human attainment. These immortals then retransmit the scriptures to human avatars. Ko Hsüan was ranked as one of these realized adepts or immortals, and Ling-pao legend records that he received thirty-three such scrolls. He is a source of a revealed tradition that eventually, after much doctrinal evolution, gave rise to religious Taoism.[18]

It is unlikely that Crowley was intellectually acquainted with Ling-pao Taoism, but like other great initiatic movements (*e.g.,* the *bodhisattvas*-on-stages of early Mahāyāna Buddhism) it agrees in

---

[17] *Ibid.,* pp. 136–137.
[18] Kohn, *op. cit.,* pp. 5–6, 43–48, 197–198.

almost every particular with his descriptions of the A∴A∴ as a trans-
æonic body of reincarnating and discarnate adepts. The A∴A∴
issued *The Book of the Law* through Crowley in 1904 E.V. It pro-
claimed a new Æon of Horus (the Egyptian god of Force and Fire)
and revealed the celestial hierarchy governing this new phase of
planetary evolution, as well as its rites and formulæ of attainment.
Crowley later received many other Holy Books,[19] and established the
A∴A∴ as a teaching and initiating order.

Crowley relished his many personæ, whether made-up, adopted
or remembered, and Ko Hsüan was no exception. An unpublished
fragment entitled "Chance?" has a fictionalized treatment of "Ko
Hsüan" that is clearly based on Crowley in New York around the
time of his Esopus Island retirement:

> On my honour, I don't know if he is a Chinaman or not. He calls
> himself Ch'ing-ching, which means "Purity and Stillness," and he
> says that he is really Ko Hsüan, that crazy drunken miracle-worker
> of the third century who upset all China with his weird practices
> and astounding feats, who said he was "Holy beyond Utterance"
> and lived for seven years in a pig-sty, as a pig does in every way,
> to prove it! [...] He is by long odds the most curious man in New
> York. [...] I found him squatted on a great divan of dull gold
> embroidery, hidden amid cushions. He was dressed in an enor-
> mous robe of the most brilliant blue, with golden symbols worked
> in thread all over it. He is entirely bald, although still young. His
> face reminded me a little of the great Napoleon, but more of Ho
> Tai, that smiling god with the huge abdomen whose image one
> sees in all the Chinese shops. His eyes, though, are amazing. They
> glint unutterable Evil, the Joy of a Devil gloating over the souls that
> he has lured to Damnation. Yet there is no cruelty in his smile; one
> would say that even Eternal Punishment seems to him but one
> more Joke.[20]

Crowley sat for a photograph (given in the frontispiece) that fits
this description of Ko Hsüan admirably, but was actually inspired by
a sly reference by his disciple Gerald J. Yorke, who wrote of Mi-Lei
Fo (Maitreya Buddha) in his memoir of China:

> That Buddha should have foreseen that this personification of
> good living would succeed him in five thousand years' time is a
> subtle jest which escaped his Indian disciples. Wise in his gen-
> eration, he realised that his message must be followed by others
> yet more vital. Chinese genius has singled out Mi-Lei, and
> enthroned him as the coming Messiah. His fat, laughing figure is

---

[19] See ΘΕΛΗΜΑ, *The Holy Books of Thelema*, in the Selected References.
[20] Unpublished MS., Yorke Collection, Warburg Institute, London.

the first to greet pilgrims as they pass the four guardians of the threshold in the outer hall of every temple. He symbolises the divine freedom to which mankind is struggling, when *the only sin will be restriction.* Alone amongst the peoples of the world the Chinese deify laughter.[21] [*Emphasis added.*]

Yorke is of course having his own "subtle jest" and paraphrasing *The Book of the Law,* which no doubt escaped his readers but delighted Crowley, a past master of the theological in-joke.

Crowley announced the *Tao Te Ching* at the back of *Little Essays Toward Truth* in 1938 but despite repeated efforts it did not appear. His successor Karl Germer tried again in the early 1960s, but his death in 1962 prevented the completion of the project. The first edition was issued by Thelema Publications in 1971, edited by Helen Parsons Smith, published in series as *The Equinox* III(8).[22]

A change made at the end of Crowley's Introduction shows that this was originally written in 1923 and revised in 1938. A postscript note in Chapter 19 shows that, while the main text was written in 1918 and the commentary in 1919, these were revised as late as 1944. The typescripts give the A∴A∴ title as *Liber LXXXI* (for its 81 chapters), but this number duplicated that of another book by Crowley (*Moonchild*) and was changed to *Liber CLVII* in 1919.[23]

In keeping with the spirit of the book, the editorial apparatus has been kept simple.[24] Works cited by Crowley, as well as relevant principal editions, appear in the Selected References.

The holograph manuscript of the *Tao Te Ching* is presumed lost, but numerous typescripts survive. The first used here incorporates Crowley's final emendations; formerly in the central O.T.O. Archives, it was sent to England for publication around 1960 and is now with the British O.T.O. Another typescript (formerly Frieda Harris') was consulted, at Pennsylvania State University Library. A third typescript in the O.T.O. Archives is identical to that used for the 1971 first edition; this lacks the final emendations but supplies variant readings and a few lacunæ in the other typescripts. Finally,

---

[21] Gerald Yorke, *China Changes* (London: Cape, 1935), pp. 147–8.

[22] Two other unauthorized editions appeared in the 1970s, edited by Stephen Skinner and Marcelo Motta. See Selected References.

[23] "Praemonstrance of A∴ A∴ ," *The Equinox* III(1) (1919), p. 15.

[24] In the *Tao Te Ching,* minor changes were made to paragraph two of the Introduction, for clarity. Several readings were adopted from the Introduction as it is reproduced in Chap. 35 of *Magick Without Tears.* Also, a few instances of eccentric punctuation were changed to parallel Crowley's usage elsewhere in a given chapter.

loose typescript material from the Yorke Collection provided the text of the A∴A∴ title page and the two brief texts (including the note signed 666) reproduced just after the Introduction. The part-titles were deleted in the revised typescript but are retained, as the Ma-wang-tui manuscripts have the order of the parts reversed. Some scholars now hold that the text properly begins with part two, and entitle it the *Te Tao Ching.* In this edition, the part-title pages are illustrated with Taoist imagery that will be suggestive to students of the Qabalah. The first is "The Empty Tao Develops into the World: The Diagram of the Great Ultimate," and the second is "The Ten Continents," which represents (with the Two Paradises) the realm where the gods and immortals dwell.

The appendix, *Liber XXI, Ch'ing-ching Ching,* was first published by the O.T.O. in London in 1939 as *Liber XXI, Khing Kang King* in a large format limited edition; some copies have original drawings on Chinese themes by Crowley. The manuscript in the Yorke Collection and the first edition were consulted for the present edition.[25]

I am grateful to Clive Harper and Benjamin Fernee of the British O.T.O. for the principal typescript; to Pennsylvania State University Special Collections for a second typescript; and to the Warburg Institute, University of London for source material. I also wish to thank Hedvig Atmer (O.T.O. Sweden) for advice on handling Chinese material; Livia Kohn of Boston University, Douglas Wile of Brooklyn College, Eva Wong of the Fung Loy Kok Taoist Temple in Denver, and Mette Sigstedt of the Swedish Museum of Far Eastern Antiquities for scholarly advice and information; Robert Kelly of Bard College for pointing the way to Esopus Island; Randall Bowyer and Robin D. Matthews for proofreading and editorial advice; and Martin P. Starr for editorial advice, research assistance and the frontispiece photograph.

Love is the law, love under will.

— HYMENAEUS BETA X°
Frater Superior, O.T.O.

---

[25] The holograph of the *Ch'ing-ching Ching* was relied upon for capitalization, as the printed edition gave the text in capitals that suited its large format but were thought too illegible for use here. A line from the manuscript title page (crediting Το Μεγα Θηριον 666) has been restored, and as noted above, the title-page original attribution to Ko Yüen or Ko Hsüan of the Wu Dynasty has been dropped. A few details of punctuation were taken from the manuscript; otherwise the text of the first edition is taken as the standard.

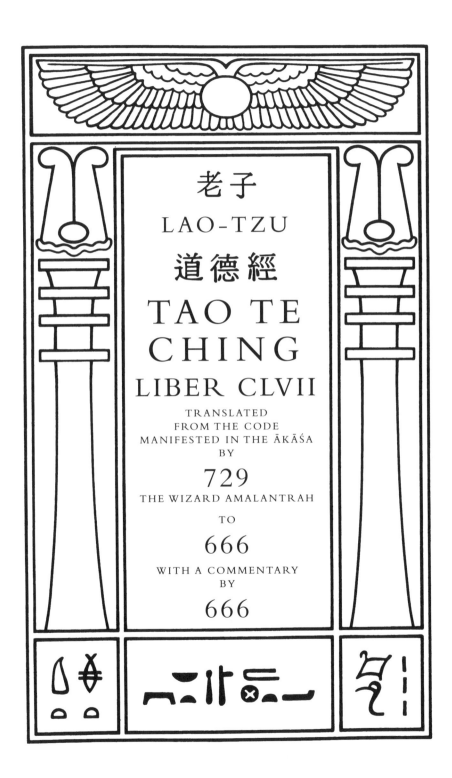

老子

LAO-TZU

道德經

TAO TE
CHING

LIBER CLVII

TRANSLATED
FROM THE CODE
MANIFESTED IN THE ĀKĀŚA
BY

729

THE WIZARD AMALANTRAH

TO

666

WITH A COMMENTARY
BY

666

A∴A∴
Publication in Class B

V.   Praemonstrator
V.V.   Imperator
S.U.A.   Cancellarius

Introduction

I BOUND MYSELF to devote my life to Magick at Easter 1898 (*era vulgari*) and received my first initiation on November 18 of that year.

My friend and climbing companion, Oscar Eckenstein, gave me my first instructions in learning the control of the mind early in 1901, in Mexico City. Srī Parānanda, Solicitor General of Ceylon (and an eminent writer upon and teacher of Yoga from the orthodox Śaivite standpoint) and Bhikkhu Ananda Metteyya (Allan Bennett, the great English Adept, who was one of my earliest instructors in Magick, and joined the Sangha in Burma in 1902), gave me my first groundings in mystical theory and practice. I spent some months of 1901 in Kandy, Ceylon, with the latter, until success crowned my work.

I also studied all varieties of Asiatic philosophy, especially with regard to the practical question of spiritual development, the Sūfī doctrines, the Upaniśads, the Saṃkhya, Vedānta, the Bhagavad-gītā and Purāṇas, the Dhammapada, and many other classics, together with numerous writings on the Tantra and Yoga of such men as Patañjali, Vivekānanda, *etc.* Not a few of these teachings are as yet wholly unknown to scholars. I made the scope of my studies as comprehensive as possible, omitting no school of thought however unimportant or repugnant.

I made a critical examination of all these teachers in the light of my practical experience. The physiological and psychological uniformity of mankind guaranteed that the diversity of expression concealed a unity of significance. This discovery was confirmed, furthermore, by reference to Jewish, Greek and Celtic traditions. One quintessential truth was common to all cults, from the Hebrides to the Yellow Sea; and even the main branches proved essentially identical. It was only the foliage that exhibited incompatibility.

When I walked across China in 1905–6, I was fully armed and accoutred by the above qualifications to attack the till-then-insoluble problem of the Chinese conception of religious truth. Practical studies of the psychology of such Mongolians as I had met in my travels, had already suggested to me that their acentric conception of the universe might represent the correspondence in consciousness of their actual psychological characteristics. I was therefore prepared to examine the doctrines of their religious and philosophical Masters without prejudice such as had always rendered nugatory the efforts of missionary Sinologists; indeed, all oriental scholars with the single exception of Rhys Davids. Until his time, translations had invariably assumed, with absurd naïveté, or (more often) arrogant bigotry, that a Chinese writer must be putting forth either a more or less distorted and degraded variation of some Christian conception, or utterly puerile absurdities. Even so great a man as Max Müller, in his introduction to the Upaniśads, seems only half inclined to admit that the apparent triviality and folly of many passages in these so-called sacred writings might owe their appearance to our ignorance of the historical and religious circumstances, a knowledge of which would render them intelligible.

During my solitary wanderings among the mountainous wastes of Yunnan, the spiritual atmosphere of China penetrated my consciousness, thanks to the absence of any intellectual impertinences from the organ of knowledge. The

Tao Te Ching revealed its simplicity and sublimity to my soul, little by little, as the conditions of my physical, no less than of my spiritual life, penetrated the sanctuaries of my spirit. The philosophy of Lao-tzu communicated itself to me, in despite of the persistent efforts of my mind to compel it to conform with my preconceived notions of what the text must mean. This process, having thus taken root in my innermost intuition during those tremendous months of wandering across Yunnan, grew continually throughout succeeding years. Whenever I found myself able once more to withdraw myself from the dissipations and distractions which contact with civilization forces upon a man, no matter how vigorously he may struggle against their insolence, to the sacred solitude of the desert, whether among the sierras of Spain or the sands of the Sahara, I found that the philosophy of Lao-tzu resumed its sway upon my soul, subtler and stronger on each successive occasion.

But neither Europe nor Africa can show any such desolation as America. The proudest, stubbornest, bitterest peasant of deserted Spain, the most primitive and superstitious Arab of the remotest oases, are a little more than kin and never less than kind at their worst; whereas in the United States one is almost always conscious of an instinctive lack of sympathy and understanding with even the most charming and cultured people. It was therefore during my exile in America that the doctrines of Lao-tzu developed most rapidly in my soul, ever forcing their way outwards until I felt it imperious, nay inevitable, to express them in terms of conscious thought.

No sooner had this resolve taken possession of me than I realized that the task approximated to impossibility. His very simplest ideas, the primitive elements of his thought, had no true correspondences in any European terminology. The very first word "Tao" presented a completely insoluble problem. It had been translated "Reason," "the Way," "TO ΩN."[1] None of these convey any true conception of the Tao.

The Tao is "Reason" in this sense, that the substance of things may be in part apprehended as being that necessary relation between the elements of thought which determines the laws of reason. In other words, the only reality is that which compels us to connect the various forms of illusion as we do. It is thus evidently unknowable, and expressible neither by speech nor by silence. All that we can know about it is that there is inherent in it a power (which however is not itself) by virtue whereof all beings appear in forms congruous with the nature of necessity.

The Tao is also "the Way"—in the following sense. Nothing exists except as a relation with other similarly postulated ideas. Nothing can be known in itself, but only as one of the participants in a series of events. Reality is therefore in the motion, not in the things moved. We cannot apprehend anything except as one postulated element of an observed impression of change.

We may express this in other terms as follows. Our knowledge of anything is in reality the sum of our observations of its successive movements, that is to say, of its path from event to event. In this sense the Tao may be translated as "the Way." It is not a thing in itself in the sense of being an object susceptible of apprehension by sense or mind. It is not the cause of any thing; it is rather the category underlying all existence or event, and therefore true and real as they are illusory, being merely landmarks invented for convenience in describing our experiences. The Tao possesses no power to cause anything to exist or to take place. Yet our experience when analyzed tells us

---

[1] [*Grk.*, "being," or "that which exists."]

that the only reality of which we may be sure is this path or Way which resumes the whole of our knowledge.

As for TO 'ΩN, which superficially might seem the best translation of Tao as described in the text, it is the most misleading of the three. For TO 'ΩN possesses an extensive connotation implying a whole system of Platonic concepts, than which nothing can be more alien to the essential quality of the Tao. Tao is neither "being" nor "not-being" in any sense which Europe could understand. It is neither existence, nor a condition or form of existence. Equally, TO MH 'ΩN[2] gives no idea of Tao. Tao is altogether alien to all that class of thought. From its connection with "that principle which necessarily underlies the fact that events occur" one might suppose that the "Becoming" of Heraclitus might assist us to describe the Tao. But the Tao is not a principle at all of that kind. To understand it requires an altogether different state of mind to any with which European thinkers in general are familiar. It is necessary to pursue unflinchingly the path of spiritual development on the lines indicated by the Sūfīs, the Hindus and the Buddhists; and, having reached the trance called *nirodha-samāpatti*, in which are destroyed all forms soever of consciousness, there appears in that abyss of annihilation the germ of an entirely new type of idea, whose principal characteristic is this: that the entire concatenation of one's previous experiences and conceptions could not have happened at all, save by virtue of this indescribable necessity.

I am only too painfully aware that the above exposition is faulty in every respect. In particular, it presupposes in the reader considerable familiarity with the subject, thus practically begging the question. It must also prove almost wholly unintelligible to the average reader, him in fact whom I especially aim to interest.

---

[2] [*Grk.*, "non-being," "that which does not exist."]

For his sake I will try to elucidate the matter by an anal-
ogy. Consider electricity. It would be absurd to say that
electricity *is* any of the phenomena by which we know it.
We take refuge in the *petitio principii*[3] of saying that electricity is that form of energy which is the principal cause of
such and such phenomena. Suppose now that we eliminate
this idea as evidently illogical. What remains? We must not
hastily answer "Nothing remains." There is some thing
inherent in the nature of consciousness, reason, perception,
sensation, and of the universe of which they inform us,
which is responsible for the fact that we observe these phenomena and not others; that we reflect upon them as we do,
and not otherwise. But, even deeper than this, part of the
reality of the inscrutable energy which determines the form
of our experience, consists in determining that experience
should take place at all. It should be clear that this has
nothing to do with any of the Platonic conceptions of the
nature of things.

The least abject asset in the intellectual bankruptcy of
European thought is the Hebrew Qabalah. Properly understood, it is a system of symbolism indefinitely elastic,
assuming no axioms, postulating no principles, asserting no
theorems, and therefore adaptable, if managed adroitly, to
describe any conceivable doctrine. It has been my continual
study since 1898, and I have found it of infinite value in the
study of the *Tao Te Ching.* By its aid I was able to attribute
the ideas of Lao-tzu to an order with which I was exceed-
ingly familiar, and whose practical worth I had repeatedly
proved by using it as the basis of the analysis and classifica-
tion of all Aryan and Semitic religions and philosophies.
Despite the essential difficulty of correlating the ideas of
Lao-tzu with any others, the persistent application of the
Qabalistic keys eventually unlocked his treasure-house. I

---

[3] [*Lat.*, as used in logic, "begging of the question."]

was able to explain to myself his teachings in terms of familiar systems.

This achievement broke the back of my Sphinx. Having once reduced Lao-tzu to Qabalistic form, it was easy to translate the result into the language of philosophy. I had already done much to create a new language based on English with the assistance of a few technical terms borrowed from Asia, and above all by the use of a novel conception of the idea of Number and of algebraic and arithmetical procedure to convey the results of spiritual experience to intelligent students.

It is therefore not altogether without confidence that I present this translation of the *Tao Te Ching* to the public. I hope and believe that careful study of the text, as elucidated by my commentary, will enable serious aspirants to the hidden Wisdom to understand (with fair accuracy) what Lao-tzu taught. It must however be laid to heart that the essence of his system will inevitably elude intellectual apprehension unless it be illuminated from above by actual living experience of the truth. Such experience is only to be attained by unswerving application to the practices which he advocates. Nor must the aspirant content himself with the mere attainment of spiritual enlightenment, however sublime. All such achievements are barren unless they be regarded as the means rather than the end of spiritual progress; allowed to infiltrate every detail of the life, not only of the spirit, but of the senses. The Tao can never be known until it interprets the most trivial actions of everyday routine. It is a fatal mistake to discriminate between the spiritual importance of meditation and playing golf. To do so is to create an internal conflict. "Let there be no difference made among you between any one thing & any other thing; for thereby there cometh hurt."[4] He who knows the

---

[4] [*Liber AL vel Legis sub figura CCXX* I:22.]

Tao knows it to be the source of all things soever; the most exalted spiritual ecstasy and the most trivial internal impression are from our point of view equally illusions, worthless masks, which hide, with grotesque painted pasteboard false and lifeless, the living face of truth. Yet, from another point of view, they are equally expressions of the ecstatic genius of truth—natural images of the reaction between the essence of one's self and one's particular environment at the moment of their occurrence. They are equally tokens of the Tao by whom, in whom, and of whom, they are. To value them for themselves is to deny the Tao and to be lost in delusion. To despise them is to deny the omnipresence of the Tao, and to suffer the illusion of sorrow. To discriminate between them is to set up the accursèd dyad, to surrender to the insanity of intellect, to overwhelm the intuition of truth, and to create civil war in the consciousness.

From 1905 to 1918, the *Tao Te Ching* was my continual study. I constantly recommended it to my friends as the supreme masterpiece of initiated wisdom, and I was as constantly disappointed when they declared that it did not impress them, especially as my preliminary descriptions of the book had aroused their keenest interest. I thus came to see that the fault lay with Legge's translation, and I felt myself impelled to undertake the task of presenting Lao-tzu in language informed by the sympathetic understanding which initiation and spiritual experience had conferred on me. During my Great Magical Retirement on Æsopus Island in the Hudson River during the summer of 1918, I set myself to this work, but I discovered immediately that I was totally incompetent. I therefore appealed to an Adept named Amalantrah, with whom I was at that time in almost daily communion. He came readily to my aid, and exhibited to me a codex of the original, which conveyed to me with absolute certitude the exact significance of the text. I was able to divine without hesitation or doubt the precise manner in which Legge had been deceived. He had translated the Chinese with singular fidelity, yet in almost every verse the interpretation was altogether misleading. There was no need to refer to the text from the point of view of scholarship. I had merely to paraphrase his translation in the light of actual knowledge of the true significance of the terms employed. Anyone who cares to take the trouble to compare the two versions will be astounded to see how slight a remodelling of a paragraph is sufficient to disperse the obstinate obscurity of prejudice, and let loose a fountain and a flood of living light; to kindle the gnarled prose of stolid scholarship into the burgeoning blossom of lyrical flame.

I completed my translation within three days, but during the last twenty years I have constantly reconsidered every sentence. The manuscript has been lent to a number of friends, scholars who have commended my work, and aspirants who have appreciated its adequacy to present the spirit of the Master's teaching. Those who had been disappointed with Legge's version were enthusiastic about mine. This circumstance is in itself sufficient to assure me that love's labour has not been lost, and to fill me with enthusiastic confidence that the present publication will abundantly contribute to the fulfillment of my True Will for which I came to earth. Let us wring from labour and sorrow the utmost of which humanity is capable. Fulfil my Will to open the portals of spiritual attainment to my fellow-men, to bring them to the enjoyment of that realization of Truth, beneath all veils of temporal falsehood, which has enlightened mine eyes and filled my mouth with song.

— ALEISTER CROWLEY

Ko Hsüan
his translation
and commentary
made during his incarnation as
Aleister Crowley
during the Great Magical Retirement
upon Æsopus Island.
Anno XIV

If any Sinologist objects to anything in this translation, let him go absorb his Yang in his own Yin, as
the Americans say, and give me credit for an original Masterpiece. Whatever Lao-tzu said or meant,
this is what I say and mean.

666.

part one

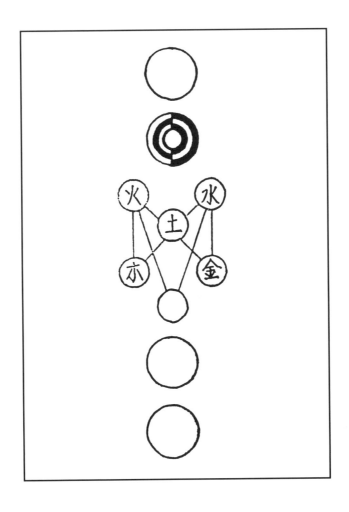

I

The Nature of the Tao

1. The Tao-Path is not the All-Tao.[1] The Name is not the Thing named.

2. Unmanifested, it is the Secret Father of Heaven ($\equiv$) and Earth ($\equiv\equiv$); manifested, it is their Mother.[2]

3. To understand this Mystery, one must be fulfilling one's will.[3] If one is not thus free, one will but gain a smattering of it.

---

[1] Tao parallels *pleroma, śiva, yod, etc.* Te parallels *logos, śakti, hé, etc.* But the conception of Lao-tzu unites all these at their highest. The best parallel is given in *Liber CCXX*, Caps. I and II, where Hadit is Tao and Nuit, Te. (Yet these are in certain aspects interchanged.) The point of this paragraph is to make discrimination or definition, not to assert the superiority of either conception. The illusion of any such preference would depend on the grade of initiation of a student. A Magus 9°=2□ of A∴A∴ would doubtless esteem the Path of "Becoming" as his Absolute, for the Law of his Grade is Change (see "Liber I vel Magi.") But—who knows?—an Ipsissimus 10°=1□ might find a conception to transcend even this. For instance, one might interpret this first paragraph as saying that Becoming is not Tao, but that Tao is a Being whose nature is Becoming. Matter and Motion cannot exist separately. The reader should regard every verse of this Book as a text worthy of the most intense and prolonged meditation. He will not understand the Book thoroughly until he has wrought his mind into its proper shape in this great Forge of *samādhi*.

[2] This doctrine is the initiated teaching to hint at which priests invented legends of parthenogenesis. (See diagram [p. 16] for precise detail.)

[3] In a moral state therefore, without desire, frictionless.

15

4. The Tao is one, and the Te but a phase thereof. The abyss of this Mystery is the Portal of Serpent-Wonder.[4]

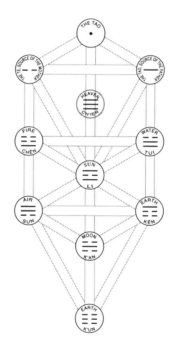

---

[4] *Cf. Berashith* for the identity of the phases "0⁰" and "something." Serpent-Wonder refers to the Magical Force called *kuṇḍalinī*.

II

The Energy-Source of the Self

1. All men know that beauty and ugliness are correlatives, as are skill and clumsiness; one implies and suggests the other.

2. So also existence and non-existence pose the one the other;[5] so also is it with ease and difficulty, length and shortness; height and lowness. Also Musick exists through harmony of opposites;[6] time and space depend upon contraposition.

3. By the use of this method the sage can fulfil his will without action, and utter his word without speech.[7]

4. All things arise without diffidence; they grow, and none interferes; they change according to their natural order, without lust of result. The work is accomplished; yet it continueth in its orbit, without goal. This work is done unconsciously; this is why its energy is indefatigable.

---

[5] *I.e.*, the thought of either implies its opposite.

[6] nay, even.

    This shows how the Tao realizes itself through its projection in correlative phases, expressing 0 as $+1 + (-1)$; to speak like a Qabalist or an electrician.

[7] Our activity is due to the incompleteness of the summing-up of Forces. Thus a man proceeds to walk "East" at four miles an hour, though he is already travelling in that direction at over 1,000 miles an hour. The end of the Meditation on Action is the realization of Hadit; wherefore any action would be a disturbance of that perfection. This being understood of the True Self, the Mind and Body proceed untrammelled in their natural path without desire on the part of the Self.

III

Quieting Folk

1. To reward merit is to stir up emulation; to prize rarities is to encourage robbery; to display desirable things is to excite the disorder of covetousness.

2. Therefore the sage governeth men by keeping their minds and their bodies at rest, contenting the one by emptiness, the other by fulness. He satisfieth their desires, thus fulfilling their wills, and making them frictionless; and he maketh them strong in body, to a similar end.

3. He delivereth them from the restlessness of knowledge and the cravings of discontent. As to those who have knowledge already, he teacheth them the way of non-action. This being assured, there is no disorder in the world.[8]

---

[8] A lecture on the Labour Problem.

IV

The Spring Without Source

1. The Tao resembleth the Emptiness of Space; to employ it, we must avoid creating ganglia. Oh Tao, how vast art Thou, the Abyss of Abysses, thou Holy and Secret Father of all Fatherhoods of Things![9]

2. Let us make our sharpness blunt;[10] let us loosen our complexes;[11] let us[12] tone down our brightness to the general obscurity. Oh Tao, how still art thou, how pure, continuous One beyond Heaven!

3. This Tao hath no Father; it is beyond all other conceptions, higher than the highest.

---

[9] See *CCXX* I:22, "Let there be no difference made among you between any one thing & any other thing". Inequality (an illusion) and disorder necessarily result from the departure from homogeneity.

[10] For sharpness implies a concentration.

[11] For these are the ganglia of thought, which must be destroyed.

[12] On the same principle.

Cf. the doctrine in *CCXX* [I:52] as to the "space-marks." The stars are blemishes, so to speak, on the continuity of Nuit.

V

The Formula of the Vacuum

1. Heaven and earth proceed without motive, but casually in their order of nature, dealing with all things carelessly, like used talismans. So also the sages deal with their people, not exercising benevolence, but allowing the nature of all to move without friction.

2. The Space between heaven and earth[13] is their breathing apparatus.[14] Exhalation is not exhaustion, but the complement of inhalation, and this equally of that. Speech[15] exhausteth; guard thyself, therefore, maintaining the perfect freedom of thy nature.

---

[13] *I.e.*, the six trigrams between ☰ and ☷.

[14] and so these must not be interfered with.

[15] by interfering with this regular order of breathing.

References to the trigrams of the *I Ching* must be explained by that Book. It would be impossible to elucidate such passages in a note. Ko Hsüan is now at work to prepare an edition of the *I*.

VI

The Perfecting of Form

1. The Te is the immortal energy of the Tao, its feminine aspect. Heaven and Earth issued from her Gate; this Gate is the Root of their World-Sycamore. Its operation is of pure Joy and Love, and faileth never.[16]

---

[16] *Cf.* in *The Book of Wisdom or Folly* [Cap. 58], the doctrine of "The Play of Nuit."

VII

The Concealment of the Light

1. Heaven and Earth are mighty in continuance, because their work is delivered from the lust of result.

2. Thus also the sage, seeking not any goal, attaineth all things; he doth not interfere in the affairs of his body, and so that body acteth without friction. It is because he meddleth not with personal aims that these come to pass with simplicity.[17]

---

[17] See *CCXX* [I:44] as to "lust of result." The general idea of the Way of the Tao is that all evil is interference. It is unnatural action which is error. Non-action is commendable only as a corrective of such; to interfere with one's own true Way is Restriction, the word of Sin.

VIII

The Nature of Peace

1. Admire thou the High Way of Water! Is not Water the soul of the life of things, whereby they change? Yet it seeketh its level, and abideth content in obscurity. So also it resembleth the Tao, in this Way thereof![18]

2. The virtue of a house is to be well-placed; of the mind, to be at ease in silence as of Space; of societies, to be well-disposed; of governments, to maintain quietude; of work, to be skilfully performed; and of all motion, to be made at the right time.[19]

3. Also it is the virtue of a man to abide in his place without discontent; thus offendeth he no man.[20]

---

[18] Hydrogen and Chlorine (for example) will not unite when perfectly dry. Dryness is immobility or death. (*Cf. The Book of Wisdom or Folly*, the doctrine concerning Change.)

[19] In all these illustrations, Lao-tzu deprecates restlessness or friction.

[20] This gives point to the previous paragraph. It is all another way of saying "Do what thou wilt."

23

IX

The Way of Reticence

1. Fill not a vessel, lest it spill in carrying. Meddle not with a sharpened point by feeling it constantly, or it will soon become blunted.[21]

2. Gold and jade endanger the house of their possessor. Wealth and honours lead to arrogance and envy, and bring ruin. Is thy way famous and thy name becoming distinguished? Withdraw, thy work once done, into obscurity; this is the way of Heaven.[22]

---

[21] Moderation. Let well alone.
[22] Attend to the work; ignore the by-products thereof.

X

Things Attainable

1. When soul[23] and body[24] are in the bond of love, they can be kept together. By concentration on the breath[25] it is brought to perfect elasticity, and one becomes as a babe.

By purifying oneself from *samādhi*, one becomes whole.[26]

2. In his dealing with individuals and with society, let him move without lust of result. In the management of his breath, let him be like the mother-bird.[27] Let his intelligence[28] comprehend every quarter; but let his knowledge[29] cease.[30]

3. Here is the Mystery of Virtue.[31] It createth all and nourisheth all; yet it doth not adhere to them; it operateth all, but knoweth not of it, nor proclaimeth it; it directeth all, but without conscious control.

---

[23] Neschamah.

[24] Nephesch.

[25] *Prāṇa.*

[26] Here we see once more the doctrine of being without friction. Internal conflict leads to rupture. Again, one's *prāṇāyāma* is to result in perfect pliability and exact adjustment to one's environment. Finally, even *sammāsamādhi* is a defect, so long as it is an experience instead of a constant state. So long as there are two to become one, there are two.

[27] *I.e.*, brooding like the Spirit, quiet, without effort. There is also a reference to a certain Legend, known in the Sanctuary of the Gnosis.

[28] Binah.

[29] Daäth.

[30] He must absorb (or understand) everything without conscious knowledge, which is a shock, implying duality, like flint and steel, while understanding is like a sponge, or even like the ocean absorbing rivers.

[31] Of the Tao and of him that hath It. Virtue—the Te.

The Value of the Unexpressed

1. The thirty spokes join in their nave, that is one; yet the wheel dependeth for use upon the hollow place for the axle. Clay is shapen to make vessels; but the contained space is what is useful. Matter is therefore of use only to mark the limits of the Space which is the thing of real value.[32]

---

[32] This introduces the doctrine of the Fourth Dimension. Matter is like the lines bounding a plane. The plane is the real thing, the lines infinitely small in comparison, and serving only to define it. So also the "Self" is an imaginary limit marking off the divisions of the "Body of God." The error of *ahaṁkāra* (the ego-making faculty) is to take the illusory surface for the Sphere. *Cf. Liber CCXX* concerning the Nature of Nuit.

XII

The Withdrawal from the External

1. The five colours film over Sight; the five sounds make Hearing dull; the five flavours conceal Taste; occupation with motion and action bedevil Mind; even as the esteem of rare things begetteth covetousness and disorder.[33]

2. The wise man seeketh therefore to content the actual needs of the people, not to excite them by the sight of luxuries. He banneth these, and concentrateth on those.[34]

---

[33] This is the regular *yogin* doctrine, and may be tested by experience of various *bhavanas* and other proper concentrations. But Lao-tzu draws a parallel for social or political use. To excite cupidity leads to theft at home, and war abroad. It is only too evident today how neglect of this rule has destroyed civilization; I need not insist on examples of how A's potash, B's iron, C's coal, and D's trade routes have caused E to set the world ablaze.

[34] The present labour troubles are due to the absurd cult of material complexities miscalled prosperity.

XIII

The Contempt for Circumstance

1. Favour and disgrace are equally to be shunned; honour and calamity to be alike regarded as adhering to the personality.[35]

2. What is this which is written concerning favour and disgrace? Disgrace is the fall from favour. He then that hath favour hath fear, and its loss begetteth fear yet greater of a further fall. What is this which is written concerning honour and calamity? It is this attachment to the body which maketh calamity possible; for were one bodiless, what evil could befall him?

3. Therefore let him that regardeth himself rightly administer also a kingdom; and let him govern it who loveth it as another man loveth himself.[36]

---

[35] And therefore "ganglia" to be loosened is written, as stated above [Chap. 4].

[36] This does not mean with extreme devotion, but rather with passionless indifference.

XIV

The Shewing-forth of the Mystery

1. We look at it, and see it not, though it is Omnipresent; and we name it the Root-Balance.[37]

We listen for it, and hear it not, though it is Omniscient; and we name it the Silence.[38]

We feel for it, and touch it not, though it is Omnipotent; and we name it the Concealed.[39]

These three Virtues hath it, yet we cannot describe it as consisting of them; but, mingling them aright, we apprehend the One.

2. Above, it shineth not; below, it is not dark. It moveth all continuously, without Expression, returning into Naught. It is the Form of That which is beyond Form; it is the Image of the Invisible; it is Change, and Without Limit.[40]

3. We confront it, and see not its Face; we pursue it, and its Back is hidden from us. Ah! but apply the Tao as in old Time to the work of the present: know it as it was known in the Beginning; follow fervently the Thread of the Tao.

---

[37] Hadit, the root of *yod*.
[38] Nuit, the root of *hé*.
[39] Ra-Hoor-Khuit, Kether, the root of *vau*.
[40] *Cf.* Ain, Ain Soph, Ain Soph Aur. Also see *The Book of Wisdom or Folly*.

XV

The Appearance of the True Nature

1. The adepts of past ages were subtle and keen to apprehend this Mystery, and their profundity was obscurity unto men. Since then they were not known, let me declare their nature.

2. To all seeming, they were fearful as men that cross a torrent in winter flood; they were hesitating like a man in apprehension of them that are about him; they were full of awe like a guest in a great house; they were ready to disappear like ice in thaw; they were unassuming like unworked wood; they were empty as a valley; and dull as the waters of a marsh.

3. Who can clear muddy water? Stillness will accomplish this. Who can obtain rest? Let motion continue equably, and it will itself be peace.

4. The adepts of the Tao, conserving its way, seek not to be actively self-conscious. By their emptiness of Self they have no need to show their youth and perfection; to appear old and imperfect is their privilege.

XVI

The Withdrawal to the Root

1. Emptiness must be perfect, and Silence made absolute with tireless strength. All things pass through the period of action; then they return to repose. They grow, bud, blossom, and fruit; then they return to the root. This return to the root is this state which we name Silence; and this Silence is Witness of their Fulfilment.

2. This cycle is the universal law. To know[41] it is the part of intelligence; to ignore it[42] bringeth folly of action, whereof the end is madness. To know it bringeth understanding and peace; and these lead to the identification of the Self with the Not-Self. This identification maketh man a king; and this kingliness groweth unto godhood. That godhood beareth fruit in the mastery of the Tao. Then the man, the Tao permeating him, endureth; and his bodily principles are in harmony, proof against decay, until the hour of his Change.

---

[41] and acquiesce in.
[42] or to rebel against it.

31

XVII

The Purity of the Current

1. In the Age of Gold, the people were not conscious of their rulers; in the Age of Silver, they loved them, with songs; in the Age of Brass, they feared them; in the Age of Iron, they despised them. As the rulers[43] lost Confidence, so also did the people lose confidence in them.

2. How hesitating did they seem, the Lords of the Age of Gold, speaking with deliberation, aware of the weight of their word! Thus they accomplished all things with success; and the people deemed their well-being to be the natural course of events.

---

[43] becoming self-conscious.

XVIII

The Decay of Manners

1. When men abandoned the Way of the Tao, benevolence and justice became necessary. Then also was need of wisdom and cunning, and all fell into illusion. When harmony ceased to prevail in the six spheres[44] it was needful to govern them by manifesting Sons.[45]

When the kingdoms and races[46] became[47] confused, loyal ministers[48] had to appear.

---

[44] The solar system.

[45] *Dhyāna-buddhas.*

[46] Elements, signs, *etc.*

[47] Self-conscious and therefore.

[48] Archangels.

It is hard at first for the student to grasp the disdain of Lao-tzu for what we call good qualities. But the need for this "good" is created by the existence of "evil," *i.e.*, the restriction of anything from doing its own will without friction. Good is then merely a symptom of evil, and so itself a poison. A man who finds Mercury and Potassium Iodide "Good" for him is a sick man. Frictionless Nourishment is the order of Change, or Life.

XIX

Returning to the Purity of the Current

1. If we forgot our statesmanship and our wisdom, it would be an hundred times better for the people. If we forgot our benevolence and our justice, they would become again like sons, folk of good will. If we forgot our machines and our business, there would be no knavery.

2. These new methods despised the olden Way, inventing fine names to disguise their barrenness. But simplicity in the doing of the will of every man would put an end to vain ambitions and desires.[49]

---

[49] Samuel Butler in *Erewhon* describes a people who had sense enough to forbid all machinery. Wells, in *The War in the Air*, prophesies the results of not doing so. At the hour of writing, An XV, ☉ in ♏ [Oct.–Nov. 1919 E.V.], we are facing the fulfilment of most of this prophecy. And still we make haste to arm!

    P.S. So also a quarter of a century later.

XX

The Withdrawal from the Common Way

1. To forget learning is to end trouble. The smallest difference in words, such as "yes" and "yea," can make endless controversy for the scholar.[50] Fearful indeed is death, since all men fear it; but the abyss of questionings, shoreless and bottomless, is worse!

2. Consider the profane man, how he preeneth himself, as if at feast, or gazing upon Spring from a tower! But as for me, I am as one who yawneth, without any trace of desire. I am like a babe before its first smile. I appear sad and forlorn, like a man homeless. The profane man hath his need filled, ay, and more also. For me, I seem to have lost all I had. My mind is as it were stupefied; it hath no definite shape. The profane man looketh lively and keen-witted; I alone appear blank in my mind. They seem eagerly critical; I appear careless and without perception. I seem to be as one adrift upon the sea, with no thought of an harbour. Profane men have, each one, his definite course of action; I alone appear useless and uncomprehending, like a man from the Border. Yea, thus I differ from all other men: but my jewel is the All-Mother.[51]

---

[50] Consider the "*homoousios - homoiousios*" quarrel of early Christianity.

[51] *Cf.* "Afloat in the æther, O my God, my God!" "Liber VII" [I:26]. It is the "aimless winging" which gives "joy ineffable" to the self-supported Absolute. [*Cf.* "Liber LXV," II:24.]

XXI

The Infinite Womb

1. The sole source of energy is the Tao. Who may declare its nature? It is beyond Sense, yet all Form is hidden within it. It is beyond Sense, yet all Perceptibles are hidden within it. It is beyond Sense, yet all Being is hidden within it. This Being excites Perception, and the Word thereof. As it was in the beginning, is now, and ever shall be, its Name[52] operateth continuously, causing all to flow in the cycle of Change, which is Love and Beauty. How do I know this? By my comprehension of the Tao.

---

[52] Te.

Zero contains all possibilities, for it may be written $0 = X + (-X)$, where X is anything soever and $-X$ its opposite. However complex X may be, it is always to be cancelled by its $-X$. Thus the universe is always potentially anything and everything, yet actually Nothing.

XXII

The Guerdon of Modesty

1. The part becometh the whole. The curve becometh straight; the void becometh full; the old becometh new. He who desireth little accomplisheth his Will with ease; who desireth many things becometh distracted.[53]

2. Therefore the sage concentrateth upon one Will, and it is as a light to the whole world. Hiding himself, he shineth; withdrawing himself, he attracteth notice; humbling himself, he is exalted; dissatisfied with himself,[54] he gaineth force to achieve his Will. Because he striveth not, no man may contend against him.

3. That is no idle saw of the men of old: "The part becometh the whole"; it is the Canon of Perfection.[55]

---

[53] Thus he hath none of them.

[54] Since the one Will is not yet attained.

[55] Any part X becomes the whole Zero, by cancelling itself through "love" of −X.

XXIII

The Void of Naught

1. To keep silence is the mark of one who is acting in full accordance with his Will. A fierce wind soon falleth; a storm-shower doth not last all day. Yet Heaven and Earth cause these; and if They fail to make violence continue, how much less can man abide in spasm of passion!

2. With him that devoteth him to Tao, the devotees of Tao are in accord; so also are the devotees of Te,[56] yea, even they who fail in seeking these are in accord.[57]

3. So then his brothers in the Tao are joyful, attaining it; and his brothers in the Te are joyful, attaining it; and they who fail in seeking these are joyful, partaking of it. But if he himself realize not the Tao with calm of confidence, then they also appear lacking in confidence.[58]

---

[56] because Te is part of Tao.

[57] because to him who has Tao all things are realized as harmonious.

[58] He who has Tao has all things rightly disposed; his own failure creates the illusion of general failure.

XXIV

Evil Manners

1. He who standeth a-tiptoe standeth not firm; he who maketh rigid his legs walketh ill. He who preeneth himself shineth not; he who talketh positively is vulgar; he who boasteth is refused acceptance; he who is wise in his own conceit is thought inferior. Such attitudes, to him that hath the view given by understanding the Tao, seem like garbage or like cancer, abhorrent to all. They then who follow the Way[59] do not admit them.

---

[59] Tao.

XXV

Images of the Mystery

1. Without Limit and Perfect, there is a Becoming, beyond Heaven and Earth. It hath nor Motion nor Form; it is alone; it changeth not;[60] it extendeth all ways; it hath no Adversary. It is like the All-Mother.

2. I know not its Name, but I call it the Tao. Moreover I exert myself, and call it Vastness.

3. Vastness, the Becoming! Becoming, it flieth afar. Afar, it draweth near. Vast is this Tao. Heaven is vast. Earth is vast. The Holy King is vast also.[61] In the Universe are Four Vastnesses, and of these is the Holy King.

4. Man followeth the[62] formula of Earth; Earth followeth that of Heaven, and Heaven that of the Tao. The Formula of the Tao is its own Nature.

---

[60] because it comprehendeth Change.
[61] for they conform to the Tao.
[62] Magick.

XXVI

The Nature of Mass

1. Mass is the fulcrum of mobility; stillness is the father of motion.

2. Therefore the sage King, though he travel afar, remaineth near his supplies. Though opportunity tempt him he remaineth quietly in proper disposition, indifferent. Should the master of an host of chariots bear himself frivolously? If he attack without support, he loseth his base; if he become a raider, he forfeiteth his throne.[63]

---

[63] This is all obvious military metaphor. If we depart from the Tao, we become engaged in futile activities which lead nowhere, and we find ourselves in the Abyss of Choronzon.

XXVII

Skill in the Method

1. The experienced traveller concealeth his tracks; the clever speaker giveth no chance to the critic; the skilled mathematician useth no abacus; the ingenious safesmith baffleth the burglar without the use of bolts, and the cunning binder without ropes and knots.[64] So also the sage, skilled in man-emancipation-craft, useth all men; understanding the value of everything, he rejecteth nothing. This is called the Occult Regimen.

2. The adept is then master to the zelator, and the zelator assisteth and honoreth the adept. Yet, unless these relations were manifest, even the most intelligent observer might be perplexed as to which was which.[65] This is called the Crown of Mystery.

---

[64] The reference is to certain "puzzles," as we should call them, common in China.

[65] The adept has become so absolutely natural that he appears unskilful. *Ars est celare artem* [*Lat.*, "it is art to conceal art"]. It is only he who has started on the Path that can divine how sublime is the Master.

XXVIII

The Return to Simplicity

1. Balance thy male strength with thy female weakness; thus shalt thou attract all things, as the ocean absorbeth all rivers; for thou shalt formulate the excellence of the Child eternal, simple, and perfect.

Knowing the Light, remain in the Dark. Manifest not thy Glory, but thine obscurity. Clothed in this Child-excellence eternal, thou hast attained the Return to the First State.

Knowing splendour of Fame, cling to Obloquy and Infamy; then shalt thou remain as in the Valley to which flow all waters, the lodestone to fascinate all men. Yea, they shall hail in thee this Excellence, eternal, simple and perfect, of the Child.

2. The raw material, wrought into form, produceth vessels.[66] So the sage king formulateth his Wholeness in divers Offices; and his Law[67] is without violence or constraint.

---

[66] Homogeneous developed into heterogeneous: 0^0 understood as "something."

[67] being concordant with the nature of his people.

XXIX

Refraining from Action

1. He that, desiring a kingdom, exerteth himself to obtain it, will fail. A kingdom is of the nature of spirit, and yieldeth not to activity. He who graspeth it, destroyeth it; he who gaineth it, loseth it.[68]

2. The wheel of nature revolveth constantly; the last becometh first, and the first last; hot things grow cold, and cold things hot; weakness overcometh strength; things gained are lost anon. Hence the wise man avoideth effort, desire, and sloth.[69]

---

[68] The usurper merely seizes the throne; the people are not with him, as with one who becomes king by virtue of natural fitness. The usurper has but the mask of power.

[69] Effort is the *rajas-guṇa*, and makes one go faster than is natural. Sloth is the *tamas-guṇa*, and makes one go slower than is natural. Desire is the disturbance of the *sattva-guṇa*, exciting the lust of Change, in one direction or the other, from the natural.

Things gained: see *Liber AL*, Cap. II, vv. 57–60.

X X X

A Warning Against War

1. If a king summon to his aid a Master of the Tao, let him not advise recourse to arms. Such action certainly bringeth the corresponding reaction.

2. Where armies are, are weeds. Bad harvests follow great hosts.

3. The good general striketh decisively, once and for all. He doth not risk[70] by overboldness. He striketh, but doth not vaunt his victory. He striketh according to strict law of necessity, not from desire of victory.

4. Things become strong and ripe, then age. This[71] is discord with the Tao; and what is not at one with the Tao soon cometh to an end.

---

[70] counter-attack.

   In other words, he acts according to the rules of the game, without losing his head by vainglory, ambition, or hatred.

[71] forcing-on of strength, instead of allowing natural growth.

XXXI

Composing Quarrel

1. Arms, though they may be beautiful, are of ill omen, abominable to all created beings. They who have the Tao love not their use.

2. The place of honour is on the right in wartime: so thinketh the man of distinction. Sharp weapons are ill-omened, unworthy of such a man; he useth them only in necessity. He valueth peace and ease, desireth not violence of victory. To desire victory is to desire the death of men; and to desire that is to fail to propitiate the people.

3. At feasts, the left hand is the high seat; at funerals, the right. The second in command of the army leadeth the left wing, the commander-in-chief, the right wing; it is as if the battle were a rite of mourning! He that hath slain most men should weep for them most bitterly; so then the place of the victor is assigned to him with philosophical propriety.

XXXII

The Wisdom of Te

1. The All-Tao[72] hath no name.

2. It is That Minute Point;[73] yet the whole world dare not contend against him that hath it. Did a lord or king gain it and guard it, all men would obey him of their own accord.

3. Heaven and Earth combining under its spell, shed forth dew,[74] extending throughout all things of its own accord, without man's interference.

4. Tao, in its phase of action, hath a name. Then men can comprehend it; when they do this, there is no more risk of wrong or ill-success.

5. As the great rivers and the oceans are to the valley streams, so is the Tao to the whole universe.

---

[72] comprehending Change within itself.

[73] Hadit.

[74] This "dew" refers to the Elixir of the Fraternity R.C., and of the O.T.O. It has been described, with proper precaution, in various passages of *The Equinox* and of *The Book of Lies*.

The Discrimination (Viveka) of Te

1. He who understandeth others understandeth Two; but he who understandeth himself understandeth One. He who conquereth others is strong; but he who conquereth himself is stronger yet.[75]

Contentment is riches; and continuous action is Will.[76]

2. He that adapteth himself perfectly to his environment, continueth for long; he who dieth without dying, liveth for ever.[77]

---

[75] for the same reason as in the first sentence.

[76] equable and carefree.

[77] The last paragraph refers once more to a certain secret practice taught by the O.T.O. See, in particular, *The Book of Lies*.

XXXIV

The Method of Attainment

1. The Tao is immanent; it extendeth to the right hand as to the left.

2. All things derive from it their being; it createth them, and all comply with it. Its work is done, and it proclaimeth it not. It is the ornament of all things, yet it claimeth not fief of them; there is nothing so small that it inhabiteth not, and informeth it.

All things return without knowledge of the Cause thereof; there is nothing so great that it inhabiteth not, and informeth it.

3. In this manner also may the Sage perform his Works. It is by not thrusting himself forward that he winneth to his success.

XXXV

The Good Will of the Te

1. The whole world is drawn to him that hath the Likeness of the Tao.[78] Men flock unto him, and suffer no ill, but gain repose, find peace, enjoy all ease.

2. Sweet sounds and cates lure the traveller from his way. But the Word of the Tao, though it appear harsh and insipid, unworthy to hearken or to behold, hath his use all inexhaustible.

---

[78] *i.e.,* the Te.

The Hiding of the Light

1. In order to draw breath, first empty the lungs; to weaken another, first strengthen him; to overthrow another, first exalt him; to despoil another, first load him with gifts; this is called the Occult Regimen.

2. The soft conquereth the hard; the weak pulleth down the strong.

3. The fish that leaveth ocean is lost; the method of government must be concealed from the people.[79]

---

[79] The single argument that can be adduced in favour of an Enlightened Democracy is that it provides more completely for the fooling of the Sovereign People than any other known system.

XXXVII

The Right Use of Government

1. The Tao proceedeth by its own nature, doing nothing; therefore there is no doing which it comprehendeth not.

2. If kings and princes were to govern in this manner, all things would operate aright by their own motion.

3. If this transmutation were my object, I should call it Simplicity.

Simplicity hath no name nor purpose; silently and at ease all things go well.

part two

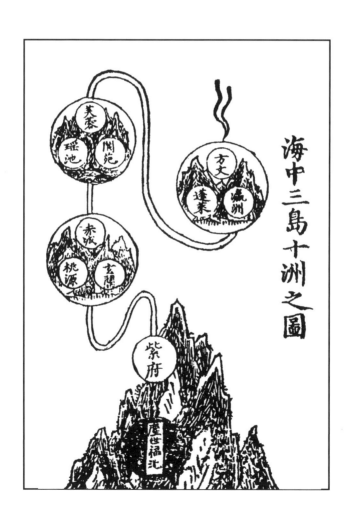

XXXVIII

Concerning the Te

1. Those who possessed perfectly the powers[80] did not manifest them, and so they preserved them. Those who possessed them imperfectly feared to lose them, and so lost them.

2. The former did nothing, nor had need to do. The latter did, and had need to do.

3. Those who possessed benevolence exercised it, and had need of it; so also was it with them who possessed justice.

4. Those who possessed the conventions displayed them; and when men would not agree, they made ready to fight them.[81]

5. Thus when the Tao was lost, the Magick Powers appeared; then, by successive degradations, came Benevolence, Justice, Convention.

6. Now convention is the shadow of loyalty and good will, and so the herald of disorder. Yea, even Understanding is but a Blossom of the Tao, and foreshadoweth Stupidity.[82]

---

[80] Te.

[81] Te appears as Chokmah-Binah, Benevolence as Chesed, Justice as Geburah, Convention as Tiphareth. Thus Kether alone is "safe"; even Chokmah-Binah risks fall unless it keeps Silence.

[82] This repeats the doctrine of the danger of Binah. The attack on Tiphareth is to be regarded as a reference to the "Fall," death of Hiram at high noon, *etc., etc.*

7. So then the Tao-Man holdeth to Mass, and avoideth Motion; he is attached to the Root, not to the flower. He leaveth the one, and cleaveth to the other.[83]

---

[83] That is, if his road be towards the Tao. In our language, he adores Nuit; but the Perfect Man, when he needs to manifest, is on the opposite curve. *Cf. The Book of Lies* [Cap. 3]: "The Brothers of A∴A∴ are Women: the Aspirants to A∴A∴ are Men."

The Law of the Beginning

1. These things have possessed the Tao from the beginning: Heaven, clear and shining; Earth, steady and easy; Spirits, mighty in Magick; Vehicles,[84] overflowing with Joy; all that hath life; and the rulers of men. All these derive their essence from the Tao.

2. Without the Tao, Heaven would dissolve,[85] Earth disrupt, Spirits become impotent, Vehicles[86] empty; living things would perish, and rulers lose their power.

3. . The root of grandeur is humility, and the strength of exaltation is its base. Thus rulers speak of themselves as "Fatherless," "Virtueless," "Unworthy," proclaiming by this that their Glory is in their shame.[87] So also the virtue of a Chariot is not any of the parts of a chariot, if they be numbered. They do not seek to appear fine like jade, but inconspicuous like common stone.[88]

---

[84] "Spirits" and "Vehicles" refer to the Lance and Cup, correlatives of Heaven and Earth.

[85] It is the invisible that is all-important: see Cap. 11.

[86] Cf. *The Questions of King Milinda*, where is the discussion of what a carriage really is.

[87] English good manners are similarly inconspicuous, and were so devised as a protection.

[88] Jade is liable to be seized and carved; ordinary stone may escape. (*Cf. Chuang-tzu* [Book IV] on the rotten tree, *etc.* [in] *Jen-chien shih* [Legge, *The Texts of Taoism*, vol. I, S.B.E. 39, p. 203].

XL

Omitting Utility

1. The Tao proceeds by correlative curves, and its might is in weakness.

2. All things arose from the Te, and the Te budded from the Tao.[89]

---

[89] The law of the Tao is constant compensation; its method is always to redress the balance, and reduce the equation to zero. In its action it resembles the form of Energy which we call gravitation very closely; it is an inertia always tending to minimize stress.

XLI

The Identity of the Differential

1. The best students, learning of the Tao, set to work earnestly to practice the Way. Mediocre students now cherish it, now let it go.

The worst students mock at it. Were it not thus mocked, it were unworthy to be Tao.

2. Thus spake the makers of Saws: the Tao at its brightest is obscure. Who advanceth in that Way, retireth. Its smooth Way is rough. Its summit is a valley. Its beauty is ugliness. Its wealth is poverty. Its virtue is vice. Its stability is change. Its form is without form. Its fulness is vacancy. Its utterance is silence. Its reality is Illusion.

3. Nameless and imperceptible is the Tao; but it informeth and perfecteth all things.

The Veils of the Tao

1. The Tao formulated the One.[90]
The One exhaled the Two.[91]
The Two were parents of the Three.[92]
The Three were parents of all things.[93]
All things pass from Obscurity to Manifestation, inspired harmoniously by the Breath of the Void.[94]

2. Men do not like to be fatherless, virtueless, unworthy; yet rulers describe themselves by these names. Thus increase bringeth decrease to some, and decrease bringeth increase to others.

3. Others have taught thus; I consent to it. Violent men and strong die not by natural death. This fact is the foundation of my Law.

---

[90] Kether or the First Æthyr.
[91] Chokmah-Binah or Yin and Yang.
[92] The second Triad.
[93] The third Triad and Malkuth.
[94] The Tao.

XLIII

The Cosmic Method

1. The softest substance[95] hunteth down the hardest;[96] the Unsubstantial[97] penetrateth where there is no opening.

Here is the Virtue of Inertia.

2. Few are they who attain: whose speech is Silence, whose Work is Inertia.

---

[95] Water — *yoni.*
[96] Rock — *liṅga.*
[97] The luminiferous ether.

XLIV

Monitorial

1. What shall it profit a man if he gain fame or wealth, and lose his life?

2. If a man cling to fame or wealth, he risketh what is worth more.

3. Be content, not fearing disgrace. Act not, and risk not criticism. Thus live thou long, without alarm.

XLV

The Overflowing of Te

1. Despise thy masterpieces; thus renew the vigour of thy creation.

Deem thy fulness emptiness; thus shall thy fulness never be empty.

Let the straight appear crooked to thee, thy Craft clumsiness; thy Musick discord.

2. Exercise moderateth cold; stillness heat. To be pure[98] and to keep silence, is the True Law of all that are beneath Heaven.

---

[98] *Brahmacharya* — Chastity in the secret Parsifal-O.T.O. sense. See also the *Ch'ing-ching Ching*. [See Appendix.]

XLVI

The Withdrawal from Ambition

1. When the Tao beareth sway on Earth, men put swift horses to night-carts. When it is neglected, they breed chargers in the border marches.

2. There is no evil worse than ambition; no misery worse than discontent; no crime greater than greed. Content of mind is peace and satisfaction eternal.

XLVII

The Vision of the Distant

1. One need not pass his threshold to comprehend all that is under Heaven, nor to look out from his lattice to behold the Tao Celestial. Nay! but the farther a man goeth, the less he knoweth.

2. The sages acquired their knowledge without travel; they named all things aright without beholding them; and, acting without aim, fulfilled their Wills.

Oblivion Overcoming Knowledge

1. The scholar seeketh daily increase of knowing; the sage of the Tao daily decrease of doing.

2. He decreaseth it, again and again, until he doth no act with the lust of result. Having attained this Inertia all accomplisheth itself.

3. He who attracteth to himself all that is under Heaven doth so without effort. He who maketh effort is not able to attract it.

XLIX

The Adaptability of the Te

1. The wise man hath no fixed principle; he adapteth his mind to his environment.

2. To the good I am good, and to the evil I am good also; thus all become good. To the true I am true, and to the false I am true; thus all become true.

3. The sage appeareth hesitating to the world, because his mind is detached. Therefore the people look and listen to him, as his children; and thus doth he shepherd them.

The Estimation of Life

1. Man cometh into life, and returneth again into death.

2. Three men in ten conserve life; three men in ten pursue death.

3. Three men also in ten desire to live, but their acts hasten their journey to the house of death. Why is this? Because of their efforts to preserve life.

4. But this have I heard. He that is wise in the economy of his life, whereof he is warden for a season, journeyeth with no need to avoid the tiger or the rhinoceros, and goeth uncorsleted among the warriors with no fear of sword or lance. The rhinoceros findeth in him no place vulnerable to its horn, the tiger to its claws, the weapon to its point. Why is this? Because there is no house of death in his whole body.

L I

The Te as the Nurse

1. All things proceed from the Tao, and are sustained by its forth-flowing virtue. Every one taketh form according to his own nature, and is perfect, each in his particular Way. Therefore each and every one of them glorify the Tao, and worship its forth-flowing Virtue.

2. This glorifying of the Tao, this worship of the Te, is constantly spontaneous, and not by appointment of Law.

3. Thus the Tao buddeth them out, nurtureth them, developeth them, sustaineth them, perfecteth them, ripeneth them, upholdeth them, and reabsorbeth them.

4. It buddeth them forth, and claimeth not lordship over them; is overseer of their changes, and boasteth not of his puissance; perfecteth them, and interfereth not with their Ways; this is called the Mystery of its Virtue.

LII

The Withdrawal into the Silence

1. The Tao buddeth forth all things under Heaven; it is the Mother of all.

2. Knowing the Mother, we may know her offspring. He that knoweth this Mother, and abideth in Her nature, remaineth in surety all his days.

3. With the mouth closed, and the Gates of Breath controlled, he remaineth at ease all his days. With the mouth open, and the Breath directed to outward affairs, he hath no surety all his days.

4. To perceive that Minute Point[99] is True Vision; to maintain the Soft and Gentle[100] is True Strength.

5. Employing harmoniously the Light Within[101] so that it returneth to its Origin, one guardeth even one's body from evil, and keepeth Silence before all men.

---

[99] Hadit.

[100] Nuit.

[101] Ra-Hoor-Khuit.

Paragraphs 3–5 refer to certain technical practices, which may be studied in *Book 4*, *The Equinox* and *Liber AL vel CCXX*.

LIII

The Witness of Greed

1. Were I discovered by men, and charged with government, my first fear would be lest I should become proud.

2. The true Path is level and smooth; but men love by-paths.

3. They adorn their courts, but they neglect their fields, and leave their storehouses empty. They wear elaborate and embroidered robes; they gird themselves with sharp swords; they eat and drink with luxury; they heap up goods; they are thievish and vainglorious. All this is opposite to the Way of Tao.

LIV

The Witness of Wisdom

1. If a man plant according to the Tao it will never be uprooted; if he thus gather, it will never be lost. His sons and his sons' sons, one following another, shall honour the shrine of their ancestor.

2. The Tao, applied to oneself, strengtheneth the Body;[102] to the family, bringeth wealth;[102] to the district, prosperity;[102] to the state, great fortune.[102] Let it be the Law of the Kingdom, and all men will increase in virtue.[102]

3. Thus we observe its effect in every case, as to the person, the family, the district, the state, and the kingdom.

4. How do I know that this is thus universal under Heaven?

By experience.

.

---

[102] Te.

    Te is always the Magick Power; it need not be explained diversely as in the text.

LV

The Spell of the Mystery

1. He that hath the Magick Powers[103] of the Tao is like a young child. Insects will not sting him; beasts or birds of prey will not attack him.

2. The young child's bones are tender and its sinews are elastic, but its grasp is firm.[104] It knoweth nothing of the Union of Man and Woman, yet its Organ may be excited. This is because of its natural perfection. It will cry all day long without becoming hoarse, because of the harmony of its being.

3. He who understandeth this harmony knoweth the mystery of the Tao, and becometh a True Sage. All devices for inflaming life, for increasing the vital Breath[105] by mental effort,[106] are evil and factitious.

4. Things become strong, then age. This[107] is in discord with the Tao, and what is not at one with the Tao soon cometh to an end.

---

[103] Te.

[104] A baby can hang from a bough for a quite indefinitely long period. This is because of monkey-atavism; in other words, it is the subconscious of the child that is at work. This subconsciousness is of its true nature, therefore in accord with the Tao.

[105] *Prāṇa.*

[106] *Haṭhayoga, etc.*

[107] Forcing-on of strength instead of allowing natural growth.

LVI

The Excellence of the Mystery

1. Who knoweth the Tao keepeth Silence; he who babbleth knoweth it not.

2. Who knoweth it closeth his mouth and controlleth the Gates of his Breath. He will make his sharpness blunt; he will loosen his complexes; he will tone down his brightness to the general obscurity. This is called the Secret of Harmony.

3. He cannot be insulted either by familiarity or aversion; he is immune to ideas of gain or loss, of honour or disgrace; he is the true man, unequalled under Heaven.

LVII

The True Influence

1. One may govern a state by restriction; weapons may be used with skill and cunning; but one acquireth true command only by freedom, given and taken.

2. How am I aware of this? By experience that to multiply restrictive laws in the kingdom impoverisheth the people; the use of machines causeth disorder in state and race alike. The more men use skill and cunning, the more machines there are; and the more laws there are, the more felons there are.

3. A wise man has said this: I will refrain from doing, and the people will act rightly of their own accord; I will love Silence, and the people will instinctively turn to perfection; I will take no measures, and the people will enjoy true wealth; I will restrain ambition, and the people will attain simplicity.

LVIII

Adaptation to Environment

1. The government that exerciseth the least care serveth the people best; that which meddleth with everybody's business worketh all manner of harm. Sorrow and joy are bedfellows; who can divine the final result of either?

2. Shall we avoid restriction? Yea; restriction distorteth nature, so that even what seemeth good in it is evil. For how long have men suffered from misunderstanding of this!

3. The wise man is foursquare, and avoideth aggression; his corners do not injure others. He moveth in a straight line[108] and turneth not aside therefrom; he is brilliant,[109] but doth not blind with his brightness.[110]

---

[108] according to his Will.
[109] like a Star.
[110] because he keeps to his own orbit.

LIX

Warding the Tao

1. To balance our earthly nature and to cultivate our heavenly nature, tread the Middle Path.

2. This Middle Path alone leadeth to the Timely Return to the True Nature. This Timely Return resulteth from the constant gathering of Magick Powers.[111] With that Gathering cometh Control. This Control we know to be Without Limit;[112] and he who knoweth the Limitless may rule the state.

3. He who possesseth the Tao continueth long. He is like a plant with well-set roots and strong stems. Thus it secureth long continuance of its life.

---

[111] Te.
[112] Like the Tao.

LX

The Duty of Government

1. The government of a kingdom is like the cooking of fish.[113]

2. If the kingdom be ruled according to the Tao, the spirits of our ancestors will not manifest their Te.[114] These spirits have this Te, but will not turn it against men. It is able to hurt men; so also is the Wise King; but he doth not.

3. When these powers[115] are in accord, their Good Will produceth the Te, endowing the people therewith.

---

[113] This means, it is the simplest possible operation.

[114] *i.e.*, their magick powers, from indignation at the mischief wrought by their descendents.

[115] The spirits and the Wise King.

LXI

The Modesty of the Te

1. A state becometh powerful when it resembleth a great river, deep-seated; to it tend all the small streams under Heaven.

2. It is as with the female, that conquereth the male by her Silence. Silence is a form of Gravity.[116]

3. Thus a great state attracteth small states by meeting their views, and small states attract the great state by revering its eminence. In the first case this Silence gaineth supporters; in the second, favour.

4. The great state uniteth men and nurtureth them; the small state wisheth the good will of the great, and offereth service: thus each gaineth its advantage. But the great state must keep Silence.

---

[116] It is not that there is any "virtue" in humility; it is simply that all lines converge at the centre of the Web.

LXII

The Workings of the Tao

1. The Tao is the most exalted of all things. It is the ornament of the good, and the protection and purification of the evil.[117]

2. Its words are the fountain of honour, and its deeds the engine of achievement. It is present even in evil.

3. Though the Son of Heaven were enthroned with his three Dukes appointed to serve him, and he were offered a round symbol-of-rank as great as might fill the hands, with a team of horses to follow, this gift were not to be matched against the Tao, which might be offered by the humblest of men.

4. Why did they of old time set such store by the Tao? Because he that sought it might find it, and because it was the Purification from all evil. Therefore did all men under Heaven esteem it the most exalted of all things.

---

[117] *Cf.* "Soul of Goodness in Things Evil." [Shakespeare, *Henry V* IV, i.]

LXIII

Forethought at the Outset

1. Act without lust of result; work without anxiety; taste without attachment to flavour; esteem small things great and few things many; repel violence with gentleness.

2. Do great things while they are yet small, hard things while they are yet easy; for all things, how great or hard soever, have a beginning when they are little and easy. So thus the wise man accomplisheth the greatest tasks without undertaking anything important.

3. Who undertaketh thoughtlessly is certain to fail in attainment; who estimateth things easy findeth them hard. The wise man considereth even easy things hard, so that even hard things are easy to him.

LXIV

Attending to Details

1. It is easy to grasp what is not yet in motion, to withstand what is not yet manifest, to break what is not yet compact, to disperse what is not yet coherent. Act against things before they become visible; attend to order before disorder ariseth.

2. The tree which filleth the embrace grew from a small shoot; the tower nine-storied rose from a low foundation; the ten day journey began with a single step.

3. He who acteth worketh harm; he who graspeth findeth it a slip. The wise man acteth not, so worketh no harm; he doth not grasp, and so doth not let go. Men often ruin their affairs on the eve of success, because they are not as prudent at the end as in the beginning.

4. The wise man willeth what others do not will,[118] and valueth not things rare.[119] He learneth what others learn not, and gathereth up what they despise. Thus he is in accord with the natural course of events, and is not overbold in action.

---

[118] He does his own will, instead of aiming at a standardized goal.
[119] and so sought after by others.

LXV

The Purity of the Te

1. They of old time that were skilled in the Tao sought not to enlighten the people, but to keep them simple.

2. The difficulty of government is the vain knowledge of the people. To use cleverness in government is to scourge the kingdom; to use simplicity is to anoint it.

3. Know these things, and make them thy law and thine ensample. To possess this Law is the Secret Perfection of rule.

Profound and Extended is this Perfection; he that possesseth it is indeed contrary to the rest, but he attracteth them to full accordance.

LXVI

Putting One's Self Last

1. The oceans and the rivers attract the streams[120] by their skill in being lower than they; thus are they masters thereof. So the Wise Man, to be above men, speaketh lowly; and to precede them acteth with humility.

2. Thus, though he be above them, they feel no burden; nor, though he precede them, do they feel insulted.

3. So then do all men delight to honour him, and grow not weary of him. He contendeth not against any man; therefore no man is able to contend against him.

---

[120] as it were tribute and worship.

LXVII

The Three Jewels

1. They say, that while this Tao of mine is great, yet it is inferior. This is the proof of its greatness. If it were like anything else, its smallness would have long been known.

2. I have three jewels of price whereto I cleave: gentleness, economy, and humility.

3. That gentleness maketh me courageous, that economy generous, that humility honoured. Men of today abandon gentleness for violence, economy for extravagance, humility for pride: this is death.

4. Gentleness bringeth victory in fight; and holdeth its ground with assurance. Heaven wardeth the gentle man, by that same virtue.

LXVIII

Assimilating One's Self to Heaven

1. He that is skilled in war maketh no fierce gestures; the most efficient fighter bewareth of anger. He who conquereth refraineth from engaging in battle; he whom men most willingly obey continueth silently with his Work. So it is said: "He is mighty who fighteth not; he ruleth who uniteth with his subjects; he shineth whose will is that of Heaven."

LXIX

The Use of the Mysterious Way

1. A great strategist saith: "I dare not take the offensive; I prefer the defensive. I dare not advance an inch; I prefer to retreat a foot." Place therefore the army where there is no army; prepare for action where there is no engagement; strike where there is no conflict; advance against the enemy where the enemy is not.[121]

2. There is no error so great as to engage in battle without sufficient force. To do so is to risk losing the gentleness[122] which is beyond price. Thus when the lines actually engage, he who regretteth the necessity is the victor.

---

[121] This is quite orthodox strategy, to avoid battle where the enemy is strong, to concentrate on the weak points of his line.

[122] elasticity.

A general who is compelled to fight at any point has lost the initiative at that point.

LXX

The Difficulty of Right Apprehension

1. My words are easy to understand and to perform; but is there anyone in the world who can understand them and perform them?

2. My words derive from a creative and universal Principle, in accord with the One Law. Men, not knowing these, understand me not.

3. Few are they that understand me; therefore am I the more to be valued. The Wise Man weareth sackcloth, but guardeth his jewel in his bosom.

LXXI

The Distemper of Knowledge

1. To know, yet to know nothing, is the highest; not to know, yet to pretend to knowledge, is a distemper.

2. Painful is this distemper; therefore we shun it. The wise man hath it not. Knowing it to be bound up with Sorrow, he putteth it away from him.

LXXII

Concerning Love of Self

1. When men fear not that which is to be feared, that which they fear cometh upon them.[123]

2. Let them not live, without thought, the superficial life.[124] Let them not weary of the Spring of Life![125]

3. By avoiding the superficial life,[126] this weariness cometh not upon them.[127]

4. These things the wise man knoweth, not showeth; he loveth himself, without isolating his value.[128] He accepteth the former and rejecteth the latter.

---

[123] They should fear Restriction of their True Wills; if not, they become slaves.

[124] They must discover the True Will, and do it. See *The Book of Wisdom or Folly*.

[125] the true, subconscious Will.

[126] rational—instead of subconscious—reaction to environment.

[127] One must make a habit of doing one's True Will; at first it is irksome, because of conflict with the accidents of life.

[128] confounding the space-marks, *etc.*

LXXIII

Establishing the Law of Freedom

1. One man, daring, is executed; another, not daring, liveth. It would seem as if the one course were profitable and the other detrimental. Yet when Heaven smiteth a man, who shall assign the cause thereof? Therefore the sage is diffident.[129]

2. The Tao of Heaven contendeth not, yet it over-cometh; it is silent, yet its need is answered; it summoneth none, but all men come to it of their free will. Its method is quietness, yet its will is efficient. Large are the meshes of Heaven's Net; wide open, yet letting none escape.[130]

---

[129] This difficult passage deprecates the security afforded by worldly prudence. He who fights and runs away may get cut down by pursuing cavalry. The only way is to adapt oneself to one's environment; that is, to the Way of the Tao, which is everywhere.

[130] *Cf.* — "Though the mills of God" *etc.* [Friedrich von Logan, *Sinnegedichte*, trans. Longfellow.]

91

LXXIV

A Restraint of Misunderstanding

1. The people have no fear of death;[131] why then seek to awe them by the threat of death? If the people feared death[132] and I could put to death evil-doers, who would dare to offend?

2. There is one appointed to inflict death.[133] He who would usurp that position resembleth a hewer of wood doing the work of a carpenter. Such an one, presumptuous, will be sure to cut his own hands.

---

[131] for the meddlesome governments have made their lives intolerable.

[132] their lives being pleasant.

[133] Azrael in the lore of Islam.

This chapter is again difficult. Par. 2 shows capital punishment as interference with Heaven's privilege. Yet in Par. 1 we see the threat of it kept as a ruler's last resort. Only, this is a "fool's knot" proposal; for such punishment is effective only when the people are so happy that they fear it infinitely, so that none ever incurs it. Hence it need never be carried out.

LXXV

The Injury of Greed

1. The people suffer hunger because of the weight of taxation imposed by their rulers. This is the cause of famine.

2. The people are difficult to govern because their rulers meddle with them. This is the cause of bad government.

3. The people welcome death because the toil of living is intolerable.[134] This is why they esteem death lightly.[135]

In such a state of insecurity it is better to ignore the question of living than to set store by it.

---

[134] owing to the meddlesome, tax-increasing, Tao-neglecting rulers.

[135] and so take the risk of brigandage, *etc.*

These chapters 74 and 75 are an interpolation, describing the conditions resulting from neglect of the Tao. The last sentence is not to be taken as didactic, as though a counsel of despair. It is the climax of the lamentation.

LXXVI

A Warning Against Rigidity

1. At the birth of man he is elastic and weak; at his death, rigid and unyielding.[136] This is the common law; trees also, in their youth, are tender and supple; in their decay, hard and dry.

2. So then rigidity and hardness are the stigmata of death; elasticity and adaptability, of life.

3. He then who putteth forth strength is not victorious; even as a strong tree filleth the embrace.[137]

4. Thus the hard and rigid have the inferior place; the soft and elastic, the superior.

---

[136] unable to adapt himself to his environment.

[137] is ready for cutting, and also, unable to grow further, decays.

LXXVII

The Way of Heaven

1. The Tao of Heaven is likened to the bending of a bow, whereby the high part is brought down, and the low part raised up. The extreme is diminished, and the middle increased.

2. This is the Way of Heaven, to remove excess, and to supplement insufficiency. Not so is the way of man, who taketh away from him that hath not to give it to him that hath already excess.

3. Who can employ his own excess to the weal of all under Heaven? Only he that possesseth the Tao.

4. So the Wise Man acteth without lust of result; achieveth and boasteth not; he willeth not to proclaim his greatness.

LXXVIII

A Creed

1. Nothing in the world is more elastic and yielding than water; yet it is preeminent to dissolve things rigid and resistant; there is nothing which can match it.

2. All men know that the soft overcometh the hard, and the weak conquereth the strong; but none are able to use this law in action.

3. A wise man hath said: "He that taketh on the burden of the state is a demigod worthy of sacrificial worship; and the true King of a people is he that undertaketh the weight of their sorrows."

4. Truth appeareth paradox.

LXXIX

Truth in Covenant

1. When enemies are reconciled, there is always an aftermath of illwill. How can this be useful?

2. Therefore the Wise Man, while he keepeth his part of the record of a transaction, doth not insist on its prompt execution. He who hath the Te considereth the situation from all sides, while he who hath it not seeketh only to benefit himself.[138]

3. In the Tao of Heaven, there is no distinction of persons in its love; but it is for the True Man to claim it.

---

[138] The Magick Powers must be exerted only according to the whole Will of the Universe, without partiality.

LXXX

Isolation

1. In a little kingdom of few people it should be the order that though there were men able to do the work of ten men or five score, they should not be employed.[139] Though the people regarded death as sorrowful, yet they should not wish to go elsewhere.

2. They should have boats and wagons, yet no necessity to travel; corslets and weapons, yet no occasion to fight.

3. For communication they should use knotted cords.[140]

4. They should deem their food sweet, their clothes beautiful, their houses homes, their customs delightful.

5. There should be another state within view, so that its fowls and dogs should be heard; yet to old age, even to death, the people should hold no traffic with it.

---

[139] at this high pressure.

[140] The curse of modern society is the Press: babble of twaddle, like a drunk prostitute vomiting. One should say only things strictly necessary.

LXXXI

The Shewing-forth of Simplicity

1. True speech is not elegant; elaborate speech is not truth. Those who know do not argue; the argumentative are without knowledge. Those who have assimilated are not learned; those who are gross with learning have not assimilated.

2. The Wise Man doth not hoard. The more he giveth, the more he hath; the more he watereth, the more is he watered himself.

3. The Tao of Heaven is like an Arrow, yet it woundeth not; and the Wise Man, in all his Works, maketh no contention.

LIBER XXI

清淨經

CH'ING-
CHING
CHING

The Classic
of Purity

MADE INTO A RIME BY ME

ALEISTER
CROWLEY

ΤΟ ΜΕΓΑ ΘΗΡΙΟΝ 666

A∴A∴
Publication in Class B

V. Praemonstrator
V.V. Imperator
S.U.A. Cancellarius

Ch'ing-ching Ching

I

Lao-chün the Master said:
    Tao is, devoid of Form;
Yet Heaven and Earth are brought to birth,
    And nurtured by Its norm.

Tao hath no Will to Work;
    Yet by Its Way of Heaven
The Moon and Sun rejoice to run
    Among the Starry Seven.

Tao hath no Name; Its Word
    Is Growth, and Sustenance
To all; I aim to give It Name:
    Tao (Heaven prosper Chance!)

Tao hath twin phase, with Te:
    The Silent and the Stressed.
Of Motion, those; of these, Repose
    Sublimely manifest.

Heaven moves, pure Silence He;
    Earth rests, beneath the Strain;
Shuttle and Loom, as Word and Womb,
    Their Mystery sustain.

Pure Motion maketh Rest
    As Silence maketh Stress.
If man were still, then Heaven should thrill
    With Earth to Nothingness.

Self loveth Silence. Yea,
    But Mind distracteth it.
Mind loveth Rest; but Passions' Pest
    Allures the trembling Wit.

If man restrain desire
    His mind will cease to roll,
And mind's release allow pure peace
    Of Silence to the Soul.

The senses will not soil;
    The thought will not upstress;
Nor Poisons (Greed, Wrath, Dulness) breed
    Their triform deadliness.

Men earn not ease of Tao
    For their desires' disease;
Because their mind is not refined
    Of thought by killing these.

If one should slay desires,
    His mind and body seem
No longer his; but phantasies
    Danced in a wanton's dream.

Slay mind, slay body, slay
    The external: matter goes.
Then space remains; renew thy pains!
    Up! Front the final foes!

Slay space; then Naught abides.
    Hold not thine holy hand!
When Naught gives back before the attack,
    Serene thy Silence stand!

All's rest, devoid of mark;
    How should desires fix tooth?
When they are past, thou surely hast
    The Silence of the Truth.

Flawless that Truth and Fixed,
    Yet apt to each appeal
Nature and Sense to influence—
    The magnet to the steel!

Oh! This true Touch with all
    Elastic and exact
That yet abides above their tides—
    The Silence free from Act!

He that hath this shall come
  Little by little, a breath,
So floweth he now, to Truth of Tao,
  Wherein he vanisheth.

Men style him Lord of Tao
  Yet He hath none to lord.
Hid motive He of all that be:
  Enough for His reward!

He that can comprehend
  This Doctrine may transmit
This Sacred Tao to men that vow
  Themselves to fathom It.

II

Lao-chün the Master said:
　　The adept in skill of soul
Hath never an aim; the bungler's shame
　　Is that he gropes a goal.

Who most possess the Te
　　Conceal their magick power;
Who least possess exert their Stress
　　Seven times in every hour.

These, who cling fast to Powers,
　　Who guard them, and display
Their magick Art—they are not part
　　Of Tao nor yet of Te.

Men win not Truth of Tao
　　Because their minds are wried.
The mind uncurbed, the self's perturbed,
　　And loses tune of tide.

Lost, the external lures;
    They turn to seek it: then
All things perplex, confuse, and vex
    Those miserable men.

Disordered thoughts arise;
    Body and mind grow sick.
Disgrace and fear grow year by year
    To their climacteric.

Wild, they are tossed about
    Through Life and Death; they quiver,
Sunk in sea-stress of Bitterness,
    And lose the Tao for ever.

The true, the abiding Tao!
    Who understandeth hath;
Who hath the Tao is Here and Now
    In Silence of the Path.

Selected References

with notes on sources and further readings

1   Butler, Samuel. *Erewhon*. New York: Penguin, 1970.
2   Chuang-tzu (Zuangzi). In *The Texts of Taoism*, Parts I–II, trans. James Legge, *Sacred Books of the East*, vols. 39–40. Oxford: Clarendon Press, 1881; rpt. New York: Dover, *c.* 1990.
3   ——. *The Complete Works of Chuang Tzu*, trans. Burton Watson. New York: Columbia UP, 1968.
4   ——. *Chuang-tzu: The Seven Inner Chapters and Other Writings*, trans. A.C. Graham. London & Boston: Allen & Unwin, 1981.
5   Crowley, Aleister. [*Berashith.*] בראשית. *An Essay on Ontology with some Remarks on Ceremonial Magic*. Paris: privately printed [1903]. Reprinted in (12).
6   ——. *Book 4*. Frater Perdurabo and Soror Virakam [pseuds. for Crowley and Mary Desti], 2 vol. *Part 1, Mysticism*. London: Wieland, [1911]. *Part 2, Magick: Preliminary Remarks*. London: Wieland, [1912]; rpt., 2 vols. in 1, York Beach, ME: Weiser, 1992. Included in (7).
7   —— (with Mary Desti and Leila Waddell). [*Book 4.*] *Magick. Liber ABA. Book Four. Parts I–IV*, ed. Hymenaeus Beta. York Beach, ME: Weiser, 1994. Includes (6).
8   ——. *The Book of Lies which is also falsely called Breaks ... with an additional commentary*. Ilfracombe, UK: Haydn Press, 1962; rpt. York Beach: Weiser, 1993.
9   —— (received by). [*The Book of the Law.*] *Liber AL vel Legis sub figura CCXX*. London: O.T.O., 1938; corrected rpt. with facsimile MS., York Beach, ME: Weiser, 1993. In (7) and (20).
10   ——. *The Book of Thoth. A Short Essay on the Tarot of the Egyptians*. The Master Therion [pseud.]. *The Equinox* III(5). London: O.T.O., 1944; rpt. York Beach, ME: Weiser, 1993. Appendix B, pp. 267–8, discusses Diagram 3, "The Chinese Cosmos."
11   ——. *The Chinese Texts of Magick and Mysticism*, ed. Marcelo Motta. Nashville: Thelema Publishing Co., 1980. This volume bears the spurious series title *The Equinox* V(3).
12   ——. *The Collected Works of Aleister Crowley*. Foyers, UK: Society for the Propagation of Religious Truth, 3 vol., 1905–7; 1 vol. "traveller's ed.," 1907; rpt. Des Plaines, IL: Yogi Publication Society, [*c.* 1974], 3 vols. Includes (5).
13   ——. *The Confessions of Aleister Crowley*. Abridged edition, ed. John Symonds and Kenneth Grant. London: Cape, 1969 and New York: Hill & Wang, 1970; rpt. London and New York: Arkana, 1989.
14   ——. *I Ching* [*Yijing*]. *Liber CCXVI*, ed. Hymenaeus Beta. *The Equinox* III(7). In press. The Legge translation with Crowley's commentary. Includes the text of (18) and Crowley's 1941 E.V. commentaries to the hexagrams.
15   ——. *Khing Kang King* [*Ch'ing-ching Ching / Qingjing jing*]. *Liber XXI. The Classic of Purity*. London: O.T.O., 1939. 2nd edition, ed. Helen Parsons Smith, Kings Beach, CA: Thelema Publications, 1973.
16   ——. *Liber Aleph vel CXI. The Book of Wisdom or Folly*, ed. Karl Germer and Marcelo Motta. *The Equinox* III(6). Barstow, CA: Thelema Publishing Co., 1961; rev. 2nd edition, ed. Hymenaeus Beta. York Beach, ME: Weiser, and New York: 93 Publishing, 1991.

109

17 ————. *Magick Without Tears*, ed. Karl Germer. Hampton, NJ: Thelema Publishing Co., 1954; abridged edition, ed. I. Regardie, St. Paul: Llewellyn, 1973; rpt. Scottsdale, AZ: New Falcon, 1991. Letters 5, 6, 34 and 35 discuss Chinese philosophy; 35 reproduces his Introduction to the *Tao Te Ching*.

18 ————. [*Shih-i/Shiyi: Explanation of the Yijing*.] *Shih Yi*, ed. Helen Parsons Smith. [*The Equinox* III(7).] Oceanside, CA: Thelema Publications, 1971. The first edition of Crowley's poetic paraphrase of the *I Ching* (*Yijing*).

19 ————. [*Tao Te Ching/Daode jing*.] *The Tao Teh King. Liber CLVII*, trans. Aleister Crowley. See (27) and (28).

20 ———— (received by). [*Thelema*] ΘΕΛΗΜΑ: *The Holy Books of Thelema*, ed. Hymenaeus Alpha and Hymenaeus Beta. York Beach, ME: Weiser, 1983. *The Equinox* III(9). Corrected 2nd printing, York Beach, ME: Weiser, and New York: 93 Publishing, 1990. Includes "Liber XXVII vel Trigrammaton."

21 *The I Ching, or Book of Changes*, trans. Richard Wilhelm, English trans. Cary F. Baynes. Bollingen Series 19, Princeton: Princeton UP, 1961, rpt. 1995.

22 [*I Ching/Yijing*.] *The Yî King. The Texts of Confucianism*, Part II, trans. James Legge, *Sacred Books of the East*, vol. 16. Oxford: Clarendon Press, 1882 [2nd ed. 1899]; rpt. Delhi: Motilal Banarsidass, 1988; rpt. as *I Ching*, New York: Dover, *c.* 1990.

23 Ko Hsüan (Ge Xuan—spurious attribution). [*Ch'ing-ching Ching/Qingjing jing*, in] *The Texts of Taoism*, vol. 2, trans. James Legge, *Sacred Books of the East*, vol. 40. Oxford: Clarendon Press, 1881; rpt. Delhi: Motilal Banarsidass, 1988, and New York: Dover, *c.* 1990.

24 ————. [*Ch'ing-ching Ching/Qingjing jing*.] *Khing Kang King. Liber XXI. The Classic of Purity*. A poetic paraphrase by Aleister Crowley. See (15).

25 Kohn, Livia. *The Taoist Experience*. Albany, NY: SUNY Press, 1993. Includes the complete text of the *Ch'ing-ching Ching/Qingjing jing* in English.

26 Lao-tzu (Laozi). [*Tao Te Ching/Daode jing*, in] *The Texts of Taoism*, Part I, trans. James Legge, *Sacred Books of the East*, vol. 39. Oxford: Clarendon Press, 1881; rpt. Delhi: Motilal Banarsidass, 1988; rpt. New York: Dover, *c.* 1990.

27 ————. *The Tao Teh King*, trans. Aleister Crowley, ed. H. Parsons Smith. Oceanside, CA: Thelema Publications, 1971. *The Equinox* III(8).

28 ————. *The Tao Teh King*, trans. Aleister Crowley, ed. Stephen Skinner. London: Askin and New York: Weiser, 1974.

29 ————. *Tao Te Ching*, trans. Stephen Mitchell. New York: Harper & Row, 1988.

30 ————. [*Tao Te Ching/Daode jing*.] *Te-tao Ching. A New Translation based on the Recently Discovered Ma-wang-tui Texts*, trans. Robert G. Henricks. New York: Ballantine Books, 1992.

31 ————. [*Tao Te Ching/Daode jing*.] Michael LaFargue. *The Tao of the Tao Te Ching: A Translation and Commentary*. Albany, NY: SUNY Press, 1992.

32 ————. *Tao Te Ching. Translation of the Ma Wang Tui Manuscripts*, trans. D.C. Lau, ed. Sarah Allan. New York: Knopf, 1994.

33 [*Milinda Pānha*.] *The Questions of King Milinda*, trans. T.W. Rhys Davids. *Sacred Books of the East*, vols. 35–36. Oxford: Clarendon Press, 1890, 1894; rpt. Delhi: Motilal Banarsidass, 1988.

34 ————. *The Debate of King Milinda: An Abridgement of the Milinda Pānha*, ed. Bhikkhu Pesala. Delhi: Motilal Banarsidass, 1991.

35 Wells, H.G. *The War in the Air*. London: G. Bell and Sons, 1908.

36 Wile, Douglas. *Art of the Bedchamber. The Chinese Sexual Yoga Classics including Women's Solo Meditation Texts*. Albany, NY: SUNY Press, 1992. Discusses the *Ch'ing-ching Ching*.

37 Wong, Eva. *Cultivating Stillness: A Taoist Manual for Transforming Body and Mind*. Boston: Shambhala, 1992. Includes a translation of the *Ch'ing-ching Ching* with an alchemical commentary.

• Zuangzi, see Chuang-tzu.

Index

111